WHAT EVERY PRINCIPAL SHOULD KNOW ABOUT

CULTURAL LEADERSHIP

W9-AWO-194

WHAT EVERY PRINCIPAL SHOULD KNOW ABOUT LEADERSHIP
The 7-Book Collection

By Jeffrey Glanz

What Every Principal Should Know About Instructional Leadership

What Every Principal Should Know About Cultural Leadership

What Every Principal Should Know About Ethical and Spiritual Leadership

What Every Principal Should Know About School-Community Leadership

What Every Principal Should Know About Collaborative Leadership

What Every Principal Should Know About Operational Leadership

What Every Principal Should Know About Strategic Leadership

WHAT EVERY PRINCIPAL SHOULD KNOW ABOUT

CULTURAL
LEADERSHIP

JEFFREY GLANZ

CORWIN PRESS
A SAGE Publications Company
Thousand Oaks, California

For information:

Corwin Press
A Sage Publications Company
2455 Teller Road
Thousand Oaks, California 91320
E-mail: order@corwinpress.com

Sage Publications Ltd.
1 Oliver's Yard
55 City Road
London EC1Y 1SP
United Kingdom

Sage Publications India Pvt. Ltd.
B-42, Panchsheel Enclave
Post Box 4109
New Delhi 110 017 India

Printed in the United States of America.

Library of Congress Cataloging-in-Publication Data

Glanz, Jeffrey.
What every principal should know about cultural leadership / Jeffrey Glanz.
    p. cm.
Includes bibliographical references and index.
ISBN 1-4129-1587-2 (pbk.)
    1. School management and organization—United States. 2. School environment—United States. 3. Multicultural education—United States. 4. School principals—United States. 5. Educational change—United States. I. Title.
LB2805.G52 2006
371.2′012—dc22   2005005355

05   06   07   08   09   10   9   8   7   6   5   4   3   2   1

Acquisitions Editor:	Elizabeth Brenkus
Editorial Assistant:	Candice L. Ling
Project Editor:	Tracy Alpern
Copy Editor:	Rachel Hile Bassett
Proofreader:	Christine Dahlin
Typesetter:	C&M Digitals (P) Ltd.
Indexer:	Gloria Tierney
Cover Designer:	Rose Storey
Graphic Designer:	Scott Van Atta

Contents

To Norma Adams, Harold Gilbert, and Michael Chiradelli, who fully understood the import of cultural leadership and who were symbolic leaders in their own right.

Acknowledgments

Lee Bolman and Terrance Deal once insightfully observed that "even in schools with weak or threadbare cultures, it is usually possible to find some things worth celebrating." Those stories, values, traditions, heroes, and heroines provide a vital starting point for updating, reinvigorating, and reframing the school's identity and culture. Principals, as cultural leaders, astutely understand the vitality of a school steeped in its traditions, lore, and beliefs. These cultural defining points provide for a sense of purpose, mission, and vision for students, parents, teachers, administrators, and community members who align themselves with the school. Together, they forge a learning community of shared purpose. As managers, advocates, planners, mentors, supervisors, and above all else leaders, principals establish a conducive tone in a school building that serves as a social, cultural, and philosophical bond. Principals realize that articulated and shared beliefs and values promote a positive school climate. Such a climate is an essential component of effective schooling. As cultural leaders, principals play a key role in shaping and reshaping patterns of learned behavior for engagement in the school that lead to a strong sense of community. This book and series are dedicated to all who aspire to the principalship, currently serve as principals, or have been principals. No nobler enterprise and profession exists, for educators are the ones who most contribute to shaping a school's culture.

* * * * * * * * * * * * * * * *

Thanks to my acquisitions editor, Lizzie Brenkus, for her gentle encouragement and support. I appreciated her thoughtful highlights of reviewer comments, which helped me focus my efforts during the revision process. Never dogmatic, but always keeping the book's focus in mind, Lizzie was a pleasure to work with. Many thanks also go to Robb Clouse, editorial director, who prompted me to consider a trilogy of sorts: a book about teaching, which eventuated into *Teaching 101*; a book about assistant principals, which led to *The Assistant Principal's Handbook*; and a book about principals, which resulted to my surprise in this groundbreaking series, *What Every Principal Should Know About Leadership.*

Special thanks to my wife, Lisa, without whose support such a venture would be impossible. I love you . . . at least as much as I love writing.

Corwin Press gratefully acknowledges the contributions of the following individuals:

Robin Dexter, Assistant
  Professor
College of Education
University of Wyoming
Laramie, WY

Gwen Gross, Superintendent
Manhattan Beach Unified
  School District
Manhattan Beach, CA

James Halley, Superintendent
  of Schools
North Kingstown School
  District
North Kingstown, RI

Phil Silsby, Principal
  (retired)
Belleville West High School
Belleville, IL

Paul Young, Principal,
  Author
West Elementary School
Lancaster, OH

About the Author

 **Jeffrey Glanz, EdD**, currently serves as Dean of Graduate Programs and Chair of the Department of Education at Wagner College in Staten Island, New York. He also coordinates the educational leadership program that leads to New York State certification as a principal or assistant principal. Prior to arriving at Wagner, he served as executive assistant to the president of Kean University in Union, New Jersey. Dr. Glanz held faculty status as a tenured professor in the Department of Instruction and Educational Leadership at Kean University's College of Education. He was named Graduate Teacher of the Year in 1999 by the Student Graduate Association and was also that year's recipient of the Presidential Award for Outstanding Scholarship. He served as an administrator and teacher in the New York City public schools for 20 years. Dr. Glanz has authored, coauthored, or coedited 13 books and has more than 35 peer-reviewed article publications. With Corwin Press he coauthored the best selling *Supervision That Improves Teaching* (2nd ed.) and *Supervision in Practice: Three Steps to Improve Teaching and Learning* and authored *The Assistant Principal's Handbook* and *Teaching 101: Classroom Strategies for the Beginning Teacher.* More recently he coauthored *Building Effective Learning Communities: Strategies for Leadership, Learning, & Collaboration.* Most recently, Dr. Glanz has authored the *What Every Principal Should Know About Leadership: The 7-Book Collection:*

> *What Every Principal Should Know About Instructional Leadership*
>
> *What Every Principal Should Know About Cultural Leadership*

What Every Principal Should Know About Ethical and Spiritual Leadership

What Every Principal Should Know About School-Community Leadership

What Every Principal Should Know About Collaborative Leadership

What Every Principal Should Know About Operational Leadership

What Every Principal Should Know About Strategic Leadership

Consult his Web site for additional information: http://www.wagner.edu/faculty/users/jglanz/web/

* * * * * * * * * * * * * * * *

The "About the Author" information you've just glanced at (excuse the pun . . . my name? . . . Glanz, "glance"?!) is standard author bio info you find in most books. As you'll discover if you glance at . . . I mean *read* . . . the Introduction, I want this book to be user-friendly in several ways. One of the ways is that I want to write as I would converse with you in person. Therefore, I prefer in most places to use the first person, so please excuse the informality. Although we've likely never met, we really do know each other if you think about it. We share a common passion about leadership, school building leadership to be more precise. We share many similar experiences. In an experiential, almost spiritual, sense, we have much in common. What I write about directly relates, I hope, to your lived experience. The information in this volume, as with the entire series, is meant to resonate, stir, provoke, and provide ideas about principal leadership, which is vital in order to promote excellence and achievement for all.

This traditional section of a book is titled "About the Author." The first paragraph in this section tells you what I "do," not "about" me or who I am. I won't bore you with all details "about me," but I'd like just to share one bit of info that communicates more meaningfully about "me" than the information in the first paragraph. I am (I presume like you) passionate about what I do. I love to teach, guide, mentor, learn, supervise, and lead. For me, leadership is self-preservation. Personally and professionally, I strive to do my very best, to use whatever God-given leadership talents I possess to make a difference in the lives of others. I continually strive to improve myself intellectually and socially, but also physically and spiritually. Family and community are very important to me. Building and sustaining community is integral to my professional practice. I see myself as part of a larger community of learners as we share, experience, overcome difficulties, learn from our mistakes, and in the end help others (students, colleagues, and community members) achieve their educational goals.

If any of the information in this book series touches you in any way, please feel free to contact me by using my personal e-mail address: tora.dojo@verizon.net. I encourage you to share your reactions, comments, and suggestions, or simply to relate an anecdote or two, humorous or otherwise, that may serve as "information from the field" for future editions of this work, ultimately to help others. Your input is much appreciated.

Questionnaire: Before We Get Started . . .

D irections: Using the Likert scale below, circle the answer that best represents your on-the-spot belief about each statement. The questionnaire serves as an advanced organizer of sorts for some of the key topics in this book, although items are purposely constructed in no particular order. Discussion of each topic, though, occurs within the context of relevant chapters. Responses or views to each statement are presented in a subsection following the questionnaire (this section begins "Now, let's analyze your responses . . ."). You may or may not agree with the points made, but I hope you will be encouraged to reflect on your own views. Reflective activities follow to allow for deeper analysis. Elaboration of ideas emanating from this brief activity will occur throughout the text and series. I encourage you to share reflections (yours and mine) with colleagues. I'd appreciate your personal feedback via the e-mail address I've listed in the "About the Author" section.

SA = Strongly Agree ("For the most part, yes.")
 A = Agree ("Yes, but . . .")
 D = Disagree ("No, but . . .")
SD = Strongly Disagree ("For the most part, no.")

SA   A   D   SD   1. To be effective, the principal should spend a great deal of time enhancing the culture of the school organization.

SA A D SD   2. Good principals try to build a team spirit in their schools.

SA A D SD   3. Examining practices of the former principal is an important task of a new building principal.

SA A D SD   4. I intend to encourage teachers to take initiative in solving schoolwide problems.

SA A D SD   5. I frequently recognize others (i.e., teachers, students, parents, assistant principals) for doing good work.

SA A D SD   6. I believe that shared beliefs and values among faculty and administration lead to positive school climate.

SA A D SD   7. Developing close, friendly, cooperative relations with others is important to me.

SA A D SD   8. I sometimes speak negatively about others when they are not present.

SA A D SD   9. Although I realize that I am the school leader, I also realize that I am not the only leader.

SA A D SD   10. I value and seek advice from others, including teachers.

SA A D SD   11. Conflict in a school or on a grade can be viewed as a means to promote individual and organizational learning and growth.

SA A D SD   12. I seek others' advice and input in terms of "how I am doing" as a cultural leader.

SA A D SD 13. I believe that schools exist for the children.

SA A D SD 14. A principal determines, in large measure, whether the organizational climate of a school is positive or toxic.

SA A D SD 15. Visionary leadership is solely or largely reserved for the principal.

SA A D SD 16. A leader with vision can accomplish anything.

SA A D SD 17. The principal should champion cultural diversity in the school.

SA A D SD 18. Organizational equilibrium is a major responsibility of the principal.

SA A D SD 19. Developing and sustaining a learning community is a primary aim of the principal.

SA A D SD 20. I really believe that all students can learn and that all teachers can be successful.

Before we analyze your responses, consider that cultural leadership is perhaps the most vital of all forms of leadership because it serves as the foundation for all others. A cultural leader is concerned with these areas of leadership, among others:

- Examining learned patterns of behavior via the norms, policies, and procedures of the past and paying close attention to how people are currently interacting and accomplishing their respective tasks
- Realizing the impact of these learned patterns of behaviors on school organization, teacher commitment, staff morale, student achievement, and community involvement
- Understanding that shared values and beliefs founded on participatory democracy, social justice, and individual growth are essential for creating and maintaining a non-toxic learning community
- Supporting, nurturing, and extending a learning environment that encourages critical reflection about commonly held ideas and values
- Leading others to develop shared vision and purpose
- Believing (and acting upon those beliefs) that people can forge shared meanings and successfully achieve their potential
- Affirming cultural diversity by actively combating prejudice and discrimination in every facet of schooling, and cherishing the contributions that each individual can make to the school
- Dealing with change, and even conflict, as natural consequences of one's work, and believing that constructive conflict and positive change can move the organization to higher levels of achievement
- Building and sustaining a learning community that is dynamic, resilient, evolving, and receptive to the learning imperatives of students (Roberts & Pruitt, 2003; Sergiovanni, 1994)

These ideas are fundamental, if not controversial. Consider the following reflective questions as you consider the meaning of cultural leadership:

Reflective Questions

1. Which of the belief statements above resonate the most with you?

2. Which of the views expressed above do you disagree with? Explain.

3. What does cultural leadership mean to you, and why is it so important, if it is? Explain.

4. Recall principals you have known, and consider the degree to which they served as cultural leaders. Which principals served as good cultural leaders, and what precisely did they do to support shared beliefs and values? Conversely, consider principals who have little, if any, *positive* influence on a school's culture, and explain how successful they have been as cultural leaders. In fact, I recall one principal who rarely if ever interacted with staff. She would sit in her office most of the day making announcements and writing very long memoranda (before the days of e-mail) so that teachers and staff could "obediently follow" her "rules and regulations." Clearly, she established a work environment that was distant and cold and that did not value participatory governance in any way, shape, or form. Although her actions influenced the school's culture and climate, her leadership provoked resentment and at times resistance; ultimately, her tenure as principal was short-lived. Can you think of principals who created a toxic school climate? Describe and explain their impact on teachers, parents, and students.

5. What other factors are important in order to promote positive cultural leadership? Explain how you might put these ideas into action.

* * * * * * * * * * * * * * *

Examine these quotations on culture and climate. What do they mean to you?

"The educational leader needs to have knowledge of his or her own values and the ability to translate that knowledge into action."

—Paul M. Quick and Anthony H. Normore

"A school's culture and the classroom climate are the direct results of attitudes, behavior, and interactions among teachers, administrators, parents, students, and staff."

—Edward F. DeRoche

"Leadership often involves challenging people to live up to their words, to close the gap between their espoused values and their actual behavior."

—Ronald A. Heifetz and Marty Linsky

"School culture includes values, symbols, beliefs, and shared meanings of parents, students, teachers, and others conceived as a group or community."

—Thomas J. Sergiovanni

"An effective school has a positive school climate. Students feel good about attending such a school and teachers feel good about teaching there. The entire staff works together to foster a caring attitude."

—C. A. Bartell

* * * * * * * * * * * * * * * *

Now, let's analyze your responses to the questionnaire:

1. To be effective, the principal should spend a great deal of time enhancing the culture of the school organization.

    Enhancing school culture involves attending to the environment, the values, the norms, the heroes and heroines, the rites and rituals, and the informal and formal communication networks (Owings & Kaplan, 2003). You should consider the following question not only on a daily basis, but whenever you are making some major decision or taking some major action: "What impact will this action or decision have on the school culture?" For instance, if you inform faculty as a new principal that you value shared decision making and will keep them involved in all major decisions, and then you make some major decision (e.g., adopting a new literacy program for the fifth grade) without consulting or involving faculty, your actions will speak louder than your words. Teacher morale will decline, and teachers will likely not trust your future proclamations related to shared decision making.

2. Good principals try to build a team spirit in their schools.

Yes. Schools are too complex for the old model of "do-it-yourself" leadership. Unless you intentionally seek to nurture leadership at all school levels among administration, faculty, staff, students, and parents, you will not be able to accomplish your goals. No single individual can go it alone. Cultural leadership is predicated in the following beliefs:

- *Leadership is a team responsibility and that leadership may emerge from any quarter of the school.*
- *Leadership is built, seamlessly, into the governance and instructional organization of the school.*
- *Leadership gives teachers the necessary time and decision-making authority to support each other's professional development on and across teams.*
- *Leadership supports individual professional growth and the sharing of best practice.*
- *Leadership provides regular opportunities for collegial collaboration.*
- *Leadership promotes a climate of inquiry and continuous improvement.*

Leadership is about people of different qualities working together toward a shared goal (Glanz, 2002). Leadership does not focus solely on the capacity of one person. Leadership is a broad, inclusive activity in which many work together toward a common goal. In such a cultural environment, team spirit is inevitable.

3. Examining practices of the former principal is an important task of a new building principal.

Yes. Too often the new school leader begins to chart a course for the school without appreciating and attending to the cultural norms and practices of the past. Doing so can at times be dangerous and detrimental to fostering positive school climate. Imagine the principal who comes into a school and wants to develop an enrichment program for gifted students. He immediately implements a new program without consulting with teachers in the school who have been there for years. Unless a principal examines the past, she or he cannot successfully forge a meaningful and effective educational program. A cultural leader would always first undertake a systematic, albeit uncomplicated, needs assessment. Here are four suggestions for accomplishing a needs assessment:

- Reflect by Posing Questions
  a. Does the school need a gifted program? What evidence indicates so?
  b. Has a gifted program ever been implemented before?
  c. If so, what happened to the program, and why was it discontinued?
  d. What will my new program contribute to addressing the needs of the gifted?
  e. With whom should I meet to discuss initial plans?

- Observe
    Prior to making any decision about implementing a program, "walk around" the school getting to know faculty, staff, students, and parents. Observe teachers and students at work. Observe committees in operation. How do they function? Who is in charge? Get a sense of the culture of the school. Use MBWA—"Management By Wandering Around." This doesn't mean aimless wandering, but rather purposeful observation. Examine records, school files, and student or teacher profiles. Analyze the school's strengths and weaknesses.

- Meet With Key Personnel
    Through informal and formal meetings, speak with parents, teachers, students, assistant principals, supervisors (school and district), coordinators, guidance counselors, secretarial staff, lunchroom workers, deans, and so on. Speaking with everyone accomplishes four important things:
  a. Allows others to voice their opinion or concerns about the new program
  b. Apprises them of future developments or plans
  c. Shares information with them that they may not be privy to
  d. Solicits their input and involvement

- *Establish a Needs Assessment Committee*
  Gather a volunteer team of teachers, supervisors, parents, and students to assist in researching, planning, and implementing the program.

4. I intend to encourage teachers to take initiative in solving schoolwide problems.

Doing so reflects your commitment to participatory school management and supporting an atmosphere conducive to continuous schoolwide improvement.

5. I frequently recognize others (i.e., teachers, students, parents, assistant principals) for doing good work.

Doing so reflects your commitment to developing a warm, inviting climate in which all stakeholders want to work as a team to achieve school goals.

6. I believe that shared beliefs and values among faculty and administration lead to positive school climate.

Although this statement may be true, simply sharing beliefs may not indicate a positive school climate. Toxic beliefs lead to a toxic environment. Cultural leaders articulate morally sound goals (Sergiovanni, 1992) that serve to support school cultural norms and improve student learning.

7. Developing close, friendly, cooperative relations with others is important to me.

Ditto. Although such a statement might seem obvious, not all who enter the principalship, unfortunately, value such cooperative relationships. Examine your values and beliefs, as discussed in the Introduction.

8. I sometimes speak negatively about others when they are not present.

Doing so is not advisable because it breeds resentment. Word will travel fast. I've personally relearned a lesson taught to me years ago by a mentor: Realize that whatever you tell anyone in private will eventually be heard by others, even the one you spoke about (and in a distorted, more negative version). Such behavior contributes to creating toxicity in the school environment.

9. Although I realize that I am the school leader, I also realize that I am not the only leader.

Here are some fundamental principles from my Finding Your Leadership Style: A Guide for Educators *(Glanz, 2002):*

- *Everyone can lead—in some way to some degree in a given situation at some time.*
- *All leaders are not the same—leadership styles, personality, or traits vary greatly.*
- *No one way of leading is better than another—each leader is talented in a different way.*
- *Effective leadership depends on the context—matching the right leader to a particular situation is most important.*
- *Effective organizations need all types of leaders—different leaders positioned strategically throughout a school or district can contribute greatly to organizational effectiveness.*

10. I value and seek advice from others, including teachers.

A cultural leader understands the value of seeking advice from others. Arrogance is not a quality a positive cultural leader possesses.

11. Conflict in a school or on a grade can be viewed as a means to promote individual and organizational learning and growth.

A cultural leader doesn't avoid conflict but uses it for constructive purposes.

12. I seek others' advice and input in terms of "how I am doing" as a cultural leader.

A cultural leader is acutely aware of her or his impact on school climate. Self-assessment, reflection, and improvement are activities and goals of a cultural leader.

13. I believe that schools exist for the children.

This statement also might seem obvious. After all, who might say otherwise? Cultural leaders are particularly sensitive to and about espoused theories and theories-in-use (Osterman & Kottkamp, 2004). Espoused theories are what we say we think and believe. Theories-in-use are what we do to actualize our beliefs. Too often, there's a gap between what we say we believe and our actions, which might belie our stated beliefs.

14. A principal determines, in large measure, whether the organizational climate of a school is positive or toxic.

You play a critical role in this respect, not the sole role, but a major one nonetheless.

15. Visionary leadership is solely or largely reserved for the principal.

Although it is true that your vision sets the tone for the school, a cultural leader's vision must consider the talents and aspirations of other school players, especially teachers.

16. A leader with vision can accomplish anything.

Too Pollyannaish for my tastes, but nothing substantial and enduring can occur without vision. Articulating vision alone is not sufficient, however. It's what you do with that vision to make it come to fruition that is critical.

17. The principal should champion cultural diversity in the school.

As a cultural leader, you value difference yet encourage shared traditions. You realize that fostering a school climate that affirms cultural diversity makes everyone feel proud and special. Cultural diversity must be supported from the top.

18. Organizational equilibrium is a major responsibility of the principal.

Such a goal is unrealistic. See response to question 11 above and Chapter 4, "Best Practices in Promoting Cultural Diversity."

19. Developing and sustaining a learning community is a primary aim of the principal.

Cultural leadership aims to support learning for teachers, parents, administrators, and students. Learning is valued above all else. As cultural leader, you seek connections between people, socially and intellectually, at all levels in the school. At a staff meeting, you might explain, "Building a learning community is tantamount to developing a commitment to shared learning." "Together," you continue, "we must be willing to learn and grow together. A problem doesn't exist for me, but must be viewed as a shared obligation . . . how can we better understand the situation and resolve together to develop strategies, if not solutions?!"

20. I really believe that all students can learn and that all teachers can be successful.

Culturally relevant leaders believe that learning is socially constructed and culturally mediated (Jordan Irvine & Armento, 2003). Hence, all students can learn, albeit at different paces and in different ways. Similarly, all teachers can achieve success (Danielson, 2002).

As you reflect upon these ideas and assumptions about cultural leadership, share your responses to the following questions with a colleague:

Reflective Questions

1. Which of the explanations above make the most sense to you?

2. Which of the explanations above make the least sense to you? Explain why.

3. How would you build team spirit in your school? Provide examples.

4. Describe three strategies you'd employ to improve school climate.

5. Have you ever spoken negatively about anyone in school? If so, describe what impact such talk had on school climate, individually or collectively.

6. Do you fear conflict? Explain why or why not.

7. Can anyone develop into a visionary leader? Explain why or why not.

See Resource B for a more detailed survey to assess your school's climate or organizational health.

CHAPTER ONE

Introduction

"The principal is the key player in a school; from the principal, the climate of the school will come. The climate of a school is its moral feeling derived from the values that the principal advocates and makes actionable. The climate significantly impacts the culture. The culture is defined by the practices, both explicit and implicit, in which the constituents of the school are involved. . . . The climate and culture of the school impacts the type of community that a school will be. The sense of community is defined by how the relationships within the school are created, valued, sustained, and managed."

—Paul M. Quick and Anthony H. Normore

The climate or atmosphere of a school reflects the cultural norms adopted by principal and teachers. Reciprocally, climate may affect a deepening of values and beliefs shared by school constituents. Culture, or ethos, is central to school success. Culture is the glue that holds the elements of school together. *Culture* refers to patterns of learned behavior, shared meanings, and a commitment to shared values. *Climate* is the mood prevalent in a school. A school, for instance, that encourages constructivist learning theory to inform the nature of knowledge and teaching practices will provide students with opportunities to construct meanings on their own. Hands-on or active learning experiences are commonly found in such schools. Classroom climate is open and engaging as teachers encourage experimentation while employing varied and alternative teaching strategies. Students are active, moving about the classroom to work on projects with fellow students in cooperative learning groups. Organized chaos may characterize the classroom experience for these students. Constructivist pedagogy is supported by teachers and principal, who believe that people learn best constructing meanings on their own, sometimes through trial and error. These values, which sustain experiential learning, create an atmosphere in which learning becomes a spirited engagement between learner and content, where the teacher serves as a facilitator. The climate that ensues from such beliefs of how students learn best affirms and deepens school commitment to learning by doing. Hence, climate and culture are reciprocal processes that represent the essence of a classroom or a school.

Culture is made up of and shaped by the values, beliefs, and attitudes that exist among teachers, students, parents, staff, and community. Culture doesn't only affect values, it also reflects them. Also, culture is reflected in the behavioral norms, traditions, and myths of the school (Schein, 1992). The culture of a school is conveyed formally via meetings, brochures, and logos and informally through hallway, cafeteria, and faculty lounge conversations.

A school climate or environment that is safe, secure, attractive, bright, and clean, where discipline codes are enforced and hallways are pleasant, is supported by a culture that promotes a sense of respect and pride in the school. As a cultural leader, you are in a pivotal position to greatly influence the nature and extent of school culture and climate. Your actions as a cultural leader ultimately affect student achievement (Cotton, 2003).

One of the challenges you face as a new leader is to widen your lens to avoid seeing behaviors and events in isolation of the context in which they occur. Rather than viewing the school from only an organizational or structural perspective (Owens, 1995), a cultural leader engages others in discussion of core beliefs and values.

Deal and Peterson (1999) recommend several questions that give principals a way to understand a school's culture:

- How long has the school existed?
- Why was it built, and who were the first inhabitants?
- Who has had a major influence on the school's direction?
- What critical incidents occurred in the past, and how were they resolved, if at all?
- What were the preceding principals, teachers, and students like?
- What does the school's architecture convey? How is space arranged and used?
- What subcultures exist inside and outside the school?
- Who are the recognized (and unrecognized) heroes and villains in the school?
- What do people say (and think) when asked what the school stands for? What would they miss if they left?
- What events are assigned special importance?
- How is conflict typically defined? How is it handled?
- What are the key ceremonies and stories of the school?
- What do people wish for? Are there patterns to their individual dreams? (pp. 17–19)

The first thing you do as a new principal is to sense the school climate and seek to understand its culture. As Matthews and Crow (2003) explain, "All other efforts will be contingent on your understanding of what already exists" (p. 146). Once you understand both climate and culture, you can begin to frame a vision for the school. Vision can also reframe a school's culture and affect climate. However, vision cannot be built in isolation of culture and climate.

The major themes or underlying assumptions of this book and series on the principalship are as follows:

- The principal is *the* key cultural leader in the school building to promote student learning. Student learning cannot occur without mindful attention to school culture and climate. These concepts form the foundation that supports student learning. As a specially trained cultural leader, you champion the beliefs and values that encourage high achievement for all students. You realize, as cultural leader, that school climate influences student learning. You serve a vital role in order to accomplish deep, sustained, and schoolwide achievement for all students (Stolp, 1991).

• High achievement for all students is the major goal for a principal. A principal may possess charisma, increase parental participation in school activities, raise funds for the PTA, organize meaningful cultural events, or even possess great vision. However, the bottom line is that a principal first and foremost is concerned with activities that actively promote good teaching, which in turn promotes student learning. A principal cannot be considered successful unless high student achievement in academic areas is achieved.

• A principal should be familiar with the three major approaches to management and leadership: classical organizational theory, the human relations approach, and the behavioral science approach (Lunenburg & Ornstein, 2003). Taken together, they offer a variety of ways of understanding and working within the school organization. School culture and climate differ within each major approach. Learning to effect change within a school requires a principal to become familiar with specific theories of management within each approach. Although this book doesn't directly address these approaches, successful principals may use various theories to accomplish certain objectives. For instance, if a principal needs to increase motivation among faculty, an understanding of Frederic Herzberg's (1966) two-factor theory of motivation is important. Similarly, Hersey and Blanchard's (1988) situational leadership theory is essential in order to realize that each school may be at a different stage of development in terms of organizational structure and maturity. Such a perspective is important for a principal to take in order to adequately assess where to start in leading and developing an organization. Although this work doesn't specifically mention each theory, many ideas are culled from the three theories (see, e.g., Argyris, 1957; Bennis, 1989; Blau & Meyer, 1987; Etzioni, 1975; Fiedler & Chemers, 1984; Maslow, 1970; Rogers, 1951; Whyte, 1956).

• The principal must play an active, ongoing role in cultural leadership. The comprehensive study *Making Sense of Leading Schools: A Study of the School Principalship* (Portin, 2003) indicated that principals do not necessarily have to have expertise in all areas (e.g., instructional, cultural, managerial, human resources, strategic, external development, micropolitical leadership), but they must be master "diagnosticians," able to provide the school what it needs at the right time and in the right context. Nevertheless, I maintain that cultural leadership is qualitatively different from most other forms of leadership. Although it's difficult to separate each form of leadership from the others, because they all form an undifferentiated whole, cultural leadership can never be simply delegated to others. Every word you speak, every action you take shapes school culture and influences climate. Others help frame school culture and climate, but you, as the principal, play an active and orchestrating role.

• The relationship among school culture and climate, instructional leadership, and student achievement is strong, as reflected in Educational Leadership Constituent Council (ELCC) standard 2 below.

This book and series is also aligned with standards established by the prominent ELCC. ELCC standards are commonly accepted by most educational organizations concerned with preparing high-quality educational leaders and as such are most authoritative (Wilmore, 2002). The ELCC, an arm of the National Council for the Accreditation of Teacher Education, developed six leadership standards used widely in principal preparation. These standards formed the basis for this book and series:

1.0: Candidates who complete the program are educational leaders who have the knowledge and ability to promote the success of all students by facilitating the development, articulation, implementation, and stewardship of a school or district vision of learning supported by the school community.

*2.0: Candidates who complete the program are educational leaders who have the knowledge and ability to promote the success of all students by promoting a positive school culture, providing an effective instructional program, applying best practices to student learning, and designing comprehensive professional growth plans for staff.

3.0: Candidates who complete the program are educational leaders who have the knowledge and ability to promote the success of all students by managing the organization, operations, and resources in a way that promotes a safe, efficient, and effective learning environment.

4.0: Candidates who complete the program are educational leaders who have the knowledge and ability to promote the success of all students by collaborating with families and other community members, responding to diverse community interests and needs, and mobilizing community resources.

5.0: Candidates who complete the program are educational leaders who have the knowledge and ability to promote the success of all students by acting with integrity, fairly, and in an ethical manner.

6.0: Candidates who complete the program are educational leaders who have the knowledge and ability to promote the success of all students by understanding, responding to, and influencing the larger political, social, economic, legal, and cultural context.

* This standard is addressed in the present book.

Readers should also familiarize themselves with the Interstate School Leaders Licensure Consortium and National Association of Elementary School Principals standards (see, e.g., http://www.ccsso .org/projects/Interstate_School_Leaders_Licensure_Consortium/ and http://www.boyercenter.org/basicschool/naesp.shtml).

Another important point to make in this introduction is for you to realize that although with other forms of leadership (e.g., instructional, operational, and strategic) you must take specific actions to address them and at times you don't actually have to actively engage in them, as a cultural leader you are continually affecting school culture and climate 24-7. Your daily activities, actions, memoranda, e-mails, personal contacts, and so forth reflect, shape, and influence school culture and climate. As such, you may not realize your actions and behaviors are scrutinized closely by others. For example, you may articulate support for nonevaluative instructional supervisory practices with teachers, but do your actions reflect such beliefs? Teachers will be listening and watching closely. Similarly, parents, students, staff, and community members will pay careful attention to your actions that reflect school culture and climate, and inevitably they will make judgments about your effectiveness. Cultural leadership is therefore subtle and occurs at every moment in thought, speech, and deed.

Reflective Questions

1. Which of the themes or assumptions above make the most sense to you?

2. Which of the themes or assumptions above make the least sense to you? Explain.

3. How do you perceive your role as cultural leader? What specific actions must you take to be effective? Be specific.

4. What kind of cultural norms and climate must you nurture in order to best promote student achievement?

---

* * * * * * * * * * * * * * * *

Allow me to offer a word on chapter format and presentation of information. Information in each of the four main chapters is presented as concisely as possible to make for easy and quick reference reading. Each chapter begins with boxed material called "What You Should Know About." The box will list and briefly explain the concepts covered in each chapter. Certainly, each chapter will not cover every bit of information there is to know about a given topic, as mentioned earlier. Each chapter culls, though, essential knowledge, skills, and dispositions necessary for a successful principal.

The boxed material below summarizes seven research-based ideas about cultural leadership that should serve as checkpoints for your own progress as a cultural leader:

Seven Research-Based Findings About the Activities of a Cultural Leader

Committed to cultural leadership, good principals know, among other things, the following:

1. Supporting positive school climate is one of the most fundamentally important goals. Cotton (2003) explains, "Almost everything that the principal says and does contributes to the overall school climate" (p. 69).

2. Paying attention to rituals, ceremonies, and other symbolic actions strengthens "a sense of affiliation with the school" (Cotton, 2003, p. 69). Effective principals realize that school culture honors tradition; instills school pride; and recognizes the achievements and contributions of teachers, students, and parents.

3. Establishing a commitment to shared vision and goals is critical. Visionary leadership that emphasizes "academic goals of the school and the importance of learning" (Cotton, 2003, p. 68) is essential.

4. Communicating and maintaining high expectations for student achievement is a chief concern of a cultural leader. Cultural leaders believe that all students can learn and that all teachers can succeed. The principal affirms the potential of all students and teachers.

5. Communicating and interacting with the school community on a continuous basis is important in order to build positive relationships. Such relationships positively affect culture and climate.

6. Supporting risk taking among teachers improves student learning. Good principals encourage teachers to experiment and innovate.

7. Maintaining high visibility and accessibility is good for school climate.

SOURCE: Based on Cotton (2003).

Before I end this introduction, I want to share with my readers something about the role culture plays in shaping perceptions that others may have of you as the principal. Doing so will highlight the importance of culture and the need to pay close attention to the ways we intentionally or inadvertently contribute to shaping people's beliefs about our work. A cultural leader is sensitive to the impact that perceptions, attitudes, and values have on their work, their ability to perform effectively, and ultimately their ability to shape school climate. The principal is aware that positive school climate can affect teacher, parent, and student morale as well as play a critical role in student achievement.

Images of Principals in Film and Television

"You may sit down, Mr. O'Mally! Think you could run this school? If you could, I wouldn't be here, now would I? No one talks at my meetings—No one—You take out your pencils and write. This is an institution of learning. If you can't control it, how can you teach?! . . . and if you don't like it, Mr. Darnell, you can quit— the same goes for the rest of you. . . . This is not a damn democracy . . . my word is law. . . . There's only one boss in this place and it's me!"

"This is an office, we knock before we enter. . . . Follow the curriculum dictated by the board of education. . . . You must go along with our policies."

"I got a complaint against this pencil you sold me—it don't work." "Ohhhhh . . . what seems to be the problem?" "Every time I write with it, it gets duller, and when I sharpen it, it gets shorter. What we have here is a vicious cycle—duller, shorter, duller, shorter, I don't know what to do?" . . ."You know what they say around here. Any time something keeps getting duller and shorter, they make it the PRINCIPAL!"

Three distinct images of principals emerge after undertaking a content analysis of films and television programs since the 1950s (Glanz, 1998a). The excerpts quoted above are indicative of these three images: principal-as-autocrat, principal-as-bureaucrat, and principal-as-buffoon.

Joe Clark, classic despot in *Lean On Me*; George Grandey, stodgy administrator sitting behind a desk in *Dangerous Minds*; and Mr. Woodman, out-of-touch dullard in *Welcome Back, Mr. Kotter* are not the only ones who are depicted unfavorably in television and the movies as insecure autocrats, petty bureaucrats, and classic buffoons. My content analysis of over 35 television programs and films from 1950 to 1997 confirms the fact that an

(Continued)

overwhelming majority of principals are depicted as either autocratic, bureaucratic, or just plain silly.

An Example

Sometimes a single television show or movie depicts all three aspects of principals, as autocrats, bureaucrats, and dimwits. A made-for-TV movie, *Kidz in the Woods,* highlights a dedicated history teacher (played by Dave Thomas) who takes eight academically and emotionally troubled high school students on a summer class trip during which they retrace the Oregon Trail via wagon trains. The object of the exercise is to "show how yesterday's events can help solve today's problems." The principal, against this unorthodox experiment, is portrayed as an autocrat, a bureaucrat, and ultimately a dimwit. The vice principal, playing a vital role in the movie, is also depicted in various negative ways, at least during most of the movie. This film also demonstrates an interesting and not uncommon relationship between a male principal and a female vice principal.

Mr. Henry Dunbar, a middle-aged, conservative high school principal, confirms his role as petty bureaucrat when he chastises the renegade history teacher, Mr. Foster, the main character in this amusing made-for-TV movie. Dunbar calls Foster into his office and demands that he follow the prescribed curriculum.

Dunbar says, "What's obvious to me is that you blame me because I insist you follow my standard curriculum."

"Your standard curriculum," Foster retorts, "is substandard, and I blame you for not accepting the responsibility for teaching these kids more than is in their books."

Foster proceeds to leave Dunbar's office as the bell rings. "I gotta go . . . unless of course you want to teach my class." Dunbar, the principal, remains silent.

The principal's incompetence is not too subtly implied. The image as incompetent bureaucrat is effectively communicated. In a later scene, the vice principal is similarly portrayed as having little, if any, teaching experience. At a school board meeting, Vice Principal Felicia Duffy defends her experience by asserting "I did teach . . . for several semesters, that is."

Mr. Dunbar, determined to waylay Foster's efforts at succeeding with his innovative strategies, demands that Miss Duffy videotape the class trip as students inevitably get into trouble. Armed with this documentation, Dunbar can convince the board that he was right. Miss Duffy, aghast at the principal's deceit and unethical behavior, tries to convince her boss not to pursue this campaign. Relying on his superordinate position in the school hierarchy and employing an autocratic tactic, Dunbar tells Duffy, "You, unlike Foster, don't have tenure." Duffy reluctantly is coerced to comply.

Interestingly, Duffy, as vice principal, complies with the chicanery rather than maintaining her integrity by adhering to more ethical standards of behavior. The image of the principal as dimwit is ultimately imparted as Dunbar's plan is foiled. Once again, principals are portrayed negatively as compared to more idealistic, intelligent teachers.

Our Miss Brooks

One of the early views of a principal that demonstrates all three tendencies, autocrat-bureaucrat-dimwit, is seen in the classic 1950s series *Our Miss Brooks*. Mr. Conklin, played by Gale Gordon, is portrayed as a stern, conservative principal who is continually lampooned by Miss Brooks (played by Eve Arden), the wisecracking high school English teacher.

In the premiere episode, Miss Brooks hurries past the principal's office. "Halt!" charges Mr. Conklin, as the audience gets its first glimpse of the principal.

"I was just on my way to the cafeteria," explains Miss Brooks.

Chastising her, he says, "May I remind you that you are traversing the hallway of a public high school, not the cinder path of the Colosseum."

"I'll slow down, Sir," Miss Brooks replies.

The principal continues, "Before you go, there is something I want to talk to you about. Would you mind loping into my office?" he says sarcastically.

"But Sir," Miss Brooks protests.

"In, girl!" he shouts. Conklin's autocratic image is buttressed numerous times by his proclivity to support school regulations at all costs.

Yet despite this serious image, Mr. Conklin is continually outwitted by the clever teacher and, more often than not, becomes the target of her ridiculous and sometimes harebrained schemes. In the premiere episode, for instance, a very annoying and mischievous Miss Brooks accidentally squirts ink all over Mr. Conklin's suit. *Our Miss Brooks* clearly illustrates the image that principals can act authoritative and official yet should not be taken too seriously.

Implications

The question I'd like to briefly address is simply "What can we learn from examining images of principals in popular culture?"

(Continued)

Why are principals portrayed as "buffoons"? At first glance, such depictions may serve simply as means of comic entertainment. After all, television and film also poke fun at authority figures in many other professions. Having a sense of humor about the portrayal of such images may be warranted. Yet the unique nature or form of such satiric entertainment may point to some other insights.

Comic satire is a method employed by popular culture to transmit subtle and, often, not-so-subtle messages about, for instance, principals as figureheads representing the school establishment. Portraying principals in such comical ways communicates, in part, that even though they occupy more prestigious positions in the school hierarchy and earn more money than teachers, they are fallible and should not be taken too seriously. Teachers and students, often disempowered in the school hierarchy, are able in this manner to circumvent their subordinate status and demonstrate their autonomy by making the principal seem foolish.

What about images of principals-as-autocrats and principals-as-bureaucrats? Schools, by and large, are organized bureaucratically. Principals and other supervisors serve to support and maintain organizational rules and regulations. Images in popular culture that portray principals as autocrats and bureaucrats are not surprising, given their role expectations and responsibilities.

Perhaps, as principals, we need to at least be aware of the images that filmmakers and television producers are sending to viewers concerning the work we do in schools. We may then, for instance, counter such images by sharing with others our opposition to autocratic and bureaucratic practices.

It has been suggested that promoting an ethic of caring (Noddings, 1984) among principals may go a long way toward altering these negative views. Whether or not such an emphasis would alter the teachers', students', and filmmakers' views of principals is uncertain. What is apparent, however, is that principals sometimes contribute to their own negative image by what they do or fail to do. Principals need to demonstrate that individual needs are paramount in any effective organization. Although caring can and should be nurtured, recruiting candidates who demonstrate such qualities should be a priority. Stereotypical images of principals as humorless bureaucrats no longer suffice. These images are socially constructed and therefore can be reframed. Principals can do so by understanding the role of beliefs and values as they intersect with school climate. As cultural leaders, you play a vital role in shaping people's images of you and the image of your school.

CASE STUDY AND REFLECTIVE QUESTIONS

Dr. Roberta Rodriguez, principal of Boynton Middle School in a middle-class suburb of Chicago, is the keynote speaker at the Parent-Teacher Association's annual dinner. A dynamic, energetic visionary, Dr. Rodriguez challenges her audience to adopt her "vision for a bright new future for students at Boynton Middle School" by voting for the new inclusive education program that she has spearheaded. "All our children deserve the best," proclaims Rodriguez. "We can no longer tolerate mediocrity. Our schools are responsible to ensure that all students are given the opportunity to succeed without harmful consequences. Schools should provide similar experiences, a common set of learnings, equally effective teaching in an encouraging and nurturing classroom environment." She continues, "Since the overwhelming research and experience of many educators indicate the dangers of ability grouping, I maintain that exclusive use of ability grouping is detrimental to the academic and social development of children. Our curricula must be and will be revised to accommodate the ever-increasing needs of all students. Teachers must have high expectations for all students. We must affirm," she concludes, "what William Spady once said, 'All children can learn and succeed, but not on the same day in the same way.' It is our choice at Boynton to show the way for the district. Our belief that all children can learn must be supported by creating a caring, nurturing, high-standards educational environment for all students." The audience breaks into a spontaneous, thunderous round of applause.

Boynton Middle School (BMS) was heralded as the first middle school in the state to base its curriculum on an inclusionary model. Fifteen teachers who were trained and certified in inclusionary education were personally recruited by Dr. Rodriguez. These teachers shared the principal's deep commitment to inclusion by remaining steadfast in the belief that all children can learn at some developmentally appropriate level. Teachers possessed a critically inclusive predisposition despite their understanding that many social and political forces may impinge on their ability to provide high-quality education to all students. These teachers persisted and committed themselves to an inclusive educational and pedagogical model. Teachers, leaders in their own right and encouraged by visionary principal Roberta Rodriguez, developed several competencies for educators who believe in fostering inclusive education. First, they articulated general principles and then principles more specific to inclusion:

The teacher committed to inclusion will demonstrate these general principles:

- *An awareness to assess factors affecting development and measurement of intelligence in a society composed of dissimilar cultures*
- *An awareness of learners' values systems, environmental backgrounds, and language patterns*
- *The need to vary assessment procedures for multicultural differences*
- *A respect for and acceptance of differences in cultural background*
- *An understanding of their own prejudices and an ability to deal with them in a positive manner*

The teacher committed to inclusion will demonstrate these specific principles:

- *The ability to describe the basic areas of exceptionality and the special needs of exceptional learners*
- *The ability to perform appropriate screening and diagnostic tests, in conjunction with special education specialists, by observing objectively the behavior and performance of exceptional children*
- *The expertise to plan, modify, and/or develop instructional materials to identify and instruct learners with exceptionalities*
- *The ability to remain sensitive to the needs of exceptional learners in the classroom*
- *The ability to collaborate effectively by respecting the values and opinions of colleagues and primary caregivers*

Roberta Rodriguez explained on many occasions that inclusion is a belief system. It is a process of facilitating an educational environment that provides access to high-quality education for all students (e.g., Kochhar, West, & Taymans, 2000; McLeskey & Waldron, 2001; Wolfendale, 2000). Teachers at BMS believe that all children learning together, in the same schools and the same classrooms, with services and supports necessary so that they can all succeed is critical to a successful school. Maintaining high expectations for all students, believing in their potential, and providing needed services to fully participate are essential. They believe that no child should be demeaned or have his or her uniqueness ignored or belittled. Students with disabilities should be educated alongside students without disabilities. Special classes or removal of children from the regular education environment should occur only when the nature or severity of the disability is such that education in the regular classroom cannot be achieved satisfactorily with the use of supplementary support services (Elliott & McKenney, 1998; Morse, 2002).

Dr. Rodriguez often says that practices that are inclusionary are based on "democratic thought and are a hope for the future." This innovative principal conceived BMS as a learning community in which professional development is not a separate initiative but, rather, is built into everything that is done, "inclusionary," if you will. She realized that structuring a middle school based on inclusionary practice would lead to criticisms from some parents, students, and community members. "Anything new and forward thinking usually does," she posited to her staff. "We must persist," she proclaimed confidently.

She rallied support for her inclusion model over many months at various community forums, school board meetings, and private encounters and at the school. She attracted a competent and like-minded staff of professional educators who believed that inclusion was imperative to ensure successful schooling for all students. She encouraged long-term teachers at the school to keep an open mind about inclusion. She demonstrated to parents and students that an inclusionary model would not in any way detract from the educational experiences for students who usually excelled in school. She pointed out that research and her 25 years in education indicate enormous positive benefits of inclusion for all students.

Despite her pep rallies, Dr. Rodriguez knew that much remained to be done to convince parents and other community constituents, and even some teachers, of the benefits of inclusion. She realized that she had to alter people's perception, attitudes, and values about how education is delivered. Besides using every opportunity to speak about inclusion's benefits, she conducted community-school workshops. Dr. Rodriguez also decided to enroll her seventh-grade child at Boynton, with the superintendent's permission. She explained, "Parents will see my child in an inclusion class and will appreciate my commitment to inclusion for all children."

Reflective Questions

1. Why do you think Dr. Rodriguez is an effective cultural leader?
2. What strategies does Dr. Rodriguez incorporate to provide for cultural leadership?
3. Would any of these strategies work for you? Explain why or why not. Be specific.
4. Do you agree with her approach to cultural leadership? Explain.
5. Explain what factors would preclude or permit you to use her cultural leadership approach.
6. How did Dr. Rodriguez use symbolic leadership in the case described above?
7. What other cultural strategies could you use to gain support for your new innovation?

CHAPTER TWO

Best Practices in Sustaining Positive Organizational Climate and Culture

"The principal's contribution to the quality of the school climate is arguably a composite of all the things he or she says or does."

—Kathleen Cotton

"The culture of an organization makes clear what the organization stands for—its values, its beliefs, its true (as distinguished from its publicly stated) goals—and provides tangible ways in which individuals in the organization may personally identify with that culture."

—Robert G. Owens

C ultural leadership is about sustaining positive organizational climate and culture. To do so requires principals first and foremost to examine their own beliefs and values and identify what they deem to be a sound and nurturing school climate. Successful cultural leaders ask themselves the following questions, among others:

- What do I care about most?
- What do I passionately believe?
- What factors, incidents, or people have influenced me the most?
- How have these influences affected my leadership style?
- How have these influences contributed to forming my beliefs and values about education and leadership?
- How do children learn best?
- What is a good teacher?
- How does one promote student achievement?
- How might I build better relationships with students?
- How might I build better relationships with teachers?
- How might I build better relationships with parents?
- How might I build better relationships with the community?
- How might I show others I care?
- How might I build staff morale?
- How should a school be organized?
- What is my view of an ideal school?

Answering these questions will help you build and sustain positive school climate and culture, because you will have uncovered fundamental beliefs and values that guide your own style of leadership. Successful cultural leaders know what they want to accomplish. They keep the end in mind. They are visionary and use the symbols, traditions, and mores of a school to actualize their vision.

Consider these eight research-based factors that affect school climate. Each factor is essential for establishing a humane school climate (Fox & Boies, n.d.). The principal's role here is essential.

---

1. **Respect**—for teachers, parents, students, and others

2. **Trust**—they are honest and trustworthy; principals will not let you down

3. **High morale**—satisfaction (see below)

4. **Opportunities for input**—shared decision making

5. **Continuous academic and social growth**

6. **Cohesiveness**—things fit together

7. **School renewal**—seeking schoolwide improvement

8. **Caring**—care for others

"These qualities," says DeRoche (1987), "are essential to a productive and satisfying environment" (p. 43).

The boxed material that follows summarizes the teaching ideas highlighted in this chapter. Four important ways to sustain organizational climate and culture are highlighted: attend to nurturing positive relationships with students and teachers, encouraging an ethic of caring throughout the school, and always considering staff morale. The list is not exhaustive but is merely meant to highlight some key concepts and ideas that successful cultural leaders should know about as they go about influencing school culture and climate. Brief reflective activities follow each major concept to provoke thought on ways to implement or further understand each idea.

What You Should Know About Promoting Positive Organizational Climate and Culture

- **Building Relationships With Students**—Find ways to involve students in meaningful ways. Encourage them to take pride in their school.
- **Building Relationships With Teachers**—A positive learning culture cannot be nurtured without teacher involvement, nor can there be positive climate without satisfied teachers.

(Continued)

- **Building an Ethic of Caring**—Principals must affirm an ethic of caring as their primary mode of belief and behavior.
- **Building Staff Morale**—Rate your staff morale by the short survey below. Remember, you set the tone for school morale by what you say or do. Remain positive (not Pollyannaish, but confident and optimistic).

1. BUILDING RELATIONSHIPS WITH STUDENTS

If you are to understand the culture of your school and be able to positively influence school climate, then you must consider your student population. Who are the students who attend your school; what are their values; and what are their academic, social, and emotional needs? Principals who take the time to understand students in their school are better able to forge meaningful relationships with them. High-quality schools are those in which student needs are addressed and fulfilled. Student satisfaction goes a long way to contributing to positive school climate. So, what do you need to know about your students, and how can you nurture those important relationships so essential for good school climate?

What Do I Need to Know About My Students?

Here are some things to consider:

1. *All students have special needs.* Although we need to serve the needs of students who have been officially designated as "learning disabled," we must realize that all students have "special needs." Isn't that true? Think about your own child or a neighbor's child. Each child is unique, and each child has special needs.

2. *All students learn in different ways and at different paces.* The days when teachers simply talked and students dutifully listened are over (as if they ever really listened anyway!). Good teachers use multiple strategies and ways to reach students, because teachers know that each student processes information

differently. Some are good auditory learners, whereas others learn best through visual stimulation. Good teachers also know that students learn at different paces. Just because Charlie "gets it" immediately doesn't mean that Sally, who doesn't immediately connect, is necessarily "slower." She just may need some additional think time or special assistance.

3. *Some students may have difficulty paying attention.* Aside from those students who have serious processing problems, all students, at different times, may tune out. Think about yourself at church or at a lecture. Ask yourself, "What can teachers do to encourage students to attend to the tasks at hand?" A teacher may have to gently remind Melissa, "Can you answer that question?" or may have to restate or rephrase a question for a student.

4. *All students are motivated.* Ever hear someone say, "Well, he's just not motivated"? That is simply not true. All students are motivated, although they may not indeed be motivated to learn what you are trying to teach them. The first step is to realize that all people are driven to act in some way, and it is our task to tap into that natural motivation.

5. *Students have five basic needs that must be addressed* (Glasser, 1975):

> *Belonging*—All people have a need to belong. Students strive to fulfill their craving to belong. If they don't receive that sense of belonging at home or in school, they often resort to potentially negative ways to satisfy this need. Do students feel needed? How can you encourage them to feel part of the school?
>
> *Security*—Students need to know that your school is a place where they can feel secure and safe. They need an environment (climate) free from ridicule and violence. Is your school a pleasant environment? Is it nicely decorated? Do you greet your students each day with a smile and pleasant countenance?
>
> *Power*—All of us need to feel empowered. Do students participate in some form of schoolwide decision making? Empowered students contribute to positive school climate.

Freedom—In what ways can you encourage students to feel that they have some freedom? Perhaps you could allow them input into what gets taught or allow them to develop a special assembly or project. By promoting and supporting student freedom you will satisfy one of their innate needs.

Fun—School and fun?! Isn't that an oxymoron? How can you make your school a place where kids enjoy themselves and have fun (yes, while they learn)?

6. *Who they are makes a difference.* Your students' social, cultural, and ethnic backgrounds as well as gender may influence how others treat them and how they interact with others.

7. *They are shapers of school culture, and they affect not only classroom climate, but school climate.* Some of us pay scant attention to student culture, explaining, at best, that their activities represent a subculture that has little if any impact on the school organization. Such a position is naive and doesn't take into consideration the influence student views and behaviors have on teacher attitudes and even parent participation.

What does all this mean? Realize that all you do as principal is meant to assist students achieve their personal best, academically, socially, and emotionally. Speak with them on a daily basis, listen earnestly to their concerns, and take their advice seriously. When students feel that their needs are addressed, their satisfaction with the school will positively affect school culture and climate.

How to Build Relationships With Students

- Listen to their ideas and suggestions.
- Solicit their advice and input.
- Spend time supporting them, especially in times of crisis.
- Believe in their capacity to learn.
- Create a culture of constructive or supportive discipline with a schoolwide policy.
- Again, solicit their advice and input.
- Invite them to share problems or concerns.
- Provide positive reinforcement.

- Apologize for mistakes you make.
- Treat them with respect.

Case Example: How Not to Treat Them With Respect

You're speaking with a few students in the hallway. You ask, "How ya doing?" A teacher walks by, and you immediately divert your attention to her, ignoring the students' responses.

Reflective Questions

1. What would you specifically do to promote student satisfaction and pride in your school?
2. Why is building relationships with students so critical to building sound culture and positive school climate?

---

2. BUILDING RELATIONSHIPS WITH TEACHERS

Clearly, building strong, meaningful relationships with teachers is important to positively influence school climate. Few, if any, principals would state that doing so is not essential to school success. Yet, we find that too many teachers report that their principal is overbearing, inconsiderate, and inattentive to teacher needs. Art Blumberg (1980) once described the "cold war" that too often exists between teacher and principal. Teachers at times complain that many principals "forget what it was like to be in the classroom." Principals who take the time to understand the school from the teacher's perspective are better able to forge meaningful relationships with them. High-quality schools are ones in which teacher needs are addressed and fulfilled. Teacher satisfaction goes a long way to contributing to positive school climate. So, how can you nurture those important relationships so essential for good school climate?

> *"Leadership emerges out of vision of what the leader and the colleagues can accomplish."*
>
> —Robert J. Starratt

How Do I Know If My Teachers Are Satisfied?

Teacher Satisfaction Checklist: How many items can you honestly check off? How do you know that your observations are correct? Provide two sources of evidence to support your position.

___ Teachers enjoy coming to school.

___ Many teachers volunteer to join committees.

___ Most teachers attend holiday parties in December and end-of-the-year celebrations.

___ Teachers praise the way the school is run to others in the community.

___ Teachers don't criticize you in public.

___ Teachers have excellent attendance records.

___ Teachers report that the lines of communication between principal and teachers are open.

___ Teachers don't feel threatened or intimidated by you.

___ Teachers report that your feedback to them is timely and instructive.

___ Teachers report your willingness to encourage innovation and risk taking.

Describe other evidence you have for teacher satisfaction.

How to Build Relationships With Teachers

- Listen to their ideas and suggestions.
- Solicit their advice and input.
- Spend time supporting them, especially in times of crisis.
- Believe in their capacity to teach.
- Create a culture of constructive discipline with a school-wide policy that supports their efforts in the classroom.

- Invite them to share problems or concerns.
- Protect them from outrageous parent complaints.
- Support teachers when falsely accused by parents or others.
- Acknowledge their accomplishments publicly.
- Apologize for mistakes you make.
- Treat them with respect.

Case Example: How Not to Treat Them With Respect

You're thinking of adopting a new reading textbook series but fail to solicit the advice of teachers.

Reflective Questions

1. What would you specifically do to promote teacher satisfaction and pride in your school?

2. Why is building relationships with teachers so critical to building sound culture and positive school climate?

3. How might you build positive relationships with parents and other key community members?

---

3. BUILDING AN ETHIC OF CARING

Let's get a bit more scholarly here. In my view, few things are more important in school administration related to the principalship, given the historic legacy of the field (e.g., Beck & Murphy, 1993), than developing and nurturing an ethic of caring leadership. Sustaining an ethic of caring sends a strong message to the educational community about how principals conduct their business, so to speak. It helps dispel some of the negative notions that have plagued the field for too many years. It reshapes people's beliefs and perceptions of the principal as first and foremost a caring

> *"It is time we had a new kind of accountability in education—one that gets back to the moral basics of caring, serving, empowering, and learning."*
>
> —Michael Fullan and Andy Hargreaves

individual who puts people first, not organizational mandates. It reframes culture and communicates what is most valuable to a principal. In turn, such an ethic builds a school climate that is characterized by warmth, affability, and caring above all else.

Informed by Noddings's (1984, 1986, 1992) work on the ethic of caring, I think that framing school leadership on a radically different paradigm of "leadership as ethic of caring"—one that supports the notion that our task as principals is essentially to support and encourage teachers while nurturing children by teaching them to be caring, moral, and productive members of society—is a very useful and potentially empowering conception of school administration. As Noddings (1992) posits, "The traditional organization of schooling is intellectually and morally inadequate for contemporary society" (p. 173). Although appropriate at some point in educational history, the traditional model of bureaucratic school organization no longer is appropriate. Nurturing an "ethic of caring," principals, like teachers, realize their ultimate motive is to inspire a sense of caring, sensitivity, appreciation, and respect for human dignity of all people despite travails that pervade our society and world. Noddings (1992) makes the point, "We should educate all our children not only for competence but also for caring. Our aim should be to encourage the growth of competent, caring, loving, and lovable people" (p. xiv).

Feminist organizational theory (Blackmore, 1993; Regan, 1990) informs this "ethic of caring" by avoiding traditional conceptions of leadership. Feminist theory questions the legitimacy of the hierarchical, patriarchal, bureaucratic school organization. Challenging traditional leadership models, feminist theory encourages community building, interpersonal relationships, nurturing, and collaboration as of primary interest (Ferguson, 1984). Although much literature in the field suggests that women as educational leaders are more attuned to fostering intimate relationships that accentuate an ethic of caring (Noddings, 1992), I think that both genders are just as likely to demonstrate that they are concerned with teaching, learning, instruction, curriculum, and people. Some argue that because women "spend more time as teachers and as mothers before they become administrators, they produce more positive interactions with community and staff; they have a more democratic, inclusive, and conflict-reducing style; and they are less concerned with bureaucracy" (Marshall,

1995, p. 488). I am not convinced that the difference lies inherently in gender. I have known some rather officious, domineering women who demonstrate autocratic and bureaucratic tendencies at the same time I have worked with men who are nurturing and caring. Although women in our society and culture are more easily accepted as sensitive, sympathetic administrators and men less so, I think both genders have essentially the same capacity for caring and nurturing, which are crucial in engendering a spirit and ethic of caring.

Supportive of this feminist view of school organization, Henry (1996) explains how feminist theory opposes bureaucracy:

> The feminist approach that I have developed in this study places people before mechanical rules or bureaucratic responses. Feminism stems from a concern not just with humankind, but with all living things and their interdependence in the universe, with a view to redefining male-female and other relations away from a notion of dominance and subordination and toward the ideal of equality and interconnectedness. . . . All human beings are seen as enriched by a feminist way of seeing and relating to the world. Instead of autonomy, separation, distance, and a mechanistic view of the world, feminism values nurturing, empathy, and a caring perspective. (pp. 19, 20)

Similarly, Noddings (1992) has led a feminist critique challenging traditional conceptions of leadership by advocating an ethic of caring that will, in the words of Marshall, Patterson, Rogers, and Steele (1996) "enable schools to become caring communities that nurture all children, regardless of their race, class, or gender" (p. 276). Unlike traditional humanistic models of administration, "caring" is inclusionary, nonmanipulative, and empowering. Whereas the main objective of bureaucracy is standardization, caring inspires individual responsibility.

> [Caring] is a situation- and person-specific way of performing in the world that requires being fully and sensitively attuned to the needs of the cared for by the person caring. Caring cannot be transformed into policies mandated from above, but caring can give form and coherence to our schools. (Marshall et al., 1996, pp. 278–279)

Starratt (1991) also provides support for an ethic of caring in educational administration. According to Starratt, an administrator committed to an ethic of caring will "be grounded in the belief that the integrity of human relationships should be held sacred and that the school as an organization should hold the good of human beings within it as sacred" (p. 195).

Although defining *caring* has been difficult (Beck, 1994), scholars who have explored this topic in depth note that caring always involves, to some degree, three activities: (a) receiving the other's perspective, (b) responding appropriately to the awareness that comes from this reception, and (c) remaining committed to others and to the relationship.

To a large extent, caring involves a change in thinking patterns, belief systems, and mind-sets (culture, if you will). The "metaphor of caring" is more conducive to collaboration and cooperation, which are essential components of participatory school management.

What do caring principals do? According to Marshall et al. (1996), they

frequently develop relationships that are the grounds for motivating, cajoling, and inspiring others to excellence. Generally thoughtful and sensitive, they see nuances in people's efforts at good performance and acknowledge them; they recognize the diverse and individual qualities in people and devise individual standards of expectation, incentives, and rewards. (p. 282)

> "Leadership is a relationship. It is a relationship of influence on the capacity of others for achieving goals. We have many examples of the power of that relationship. We are also advised that it is a relationship that is continually challenged and necessarily renewed."
>
> —Michael Dickmann, Nancy Stanford-Blair, and Anthea Rosati-Bojar

These characteristics are clearly "antithetical to bureaucratic models that require standardization and uniform application of policy" (Marshall et al., 1996, p. 282). Beck (1994) agrees, noting that "caring instructional leaders would be considerate and fundamentally noncritical. With teachers, they would assume the roles of professional colleagues, co-learners, supportive counselors, and friends" (p. 93). Caring principals put people first and policy second.

Articulating a "new style of leadership," Raymond Callahan (1996) (author of *Education and the Cult of Efficiency*, 1962) emphasized the need to attract principals who "offer a [shift] from tough to caring, from controlling to motivating and communicating; and from overpowering to empowering their employees." Callahan concluded, "I think we could use more of these qualities in our schools" (p. 14).

Reflective Questions

1. What can you do as the principal to ensure that an ethic of caring is paramount?

2. Describe some caring principals you have known. What did they do differently than "less caring" ones?

3. How does an ethic of caring, more precisely, reframe culture and sustain climate?

---

4. BUILDING STAFF MORALE

Sustaining a culture of caring, for instance, and a positive climate is reflected in staff morale. You should assess the degree to which your school is characterized by high staff morale. The simple logic of the premise is that if your staff is happy, engaged, and involved in actively pursuing your vision or mission, then you have built a framework from which all else can proceed successfully.

How would you rate your staff morale according to this semantic inventory (adopted, in part, from DeRoche, 1987)?

Warm	__	__	__	__	__	Cool
	5	4	3	2	1	

Professional	__	__	__	__	__	Unprofessional
	5	4	3	2	1	

Accepting	__	__	__	__	__	Rejecting
	5	4	3	2	1	

Democratic	__	__	__	__	__	Autocratic
	5	4	3	2	1	

Cooperative	__	__	__	__	__	Competitive
	5	4	3	2	1	

Sociable	__	__	__	__	__	Unsociable
	5	4	3	2	1	

Finally, rate school morale in general:

High	__	__	__	__	__	Low
	5	4	3	2	1	

Reflective Questions

1. What evidence can you cite to support your observations about school morale?

2. Describe some specific cultural strategies you might employ to reinforce or develop high staff morale?

CONCLUSION

I have certainly not covered all aspects of sustaining climate and culture. A principal plays a critical role in shaping school culture and affecting climate. The German philosopher Arthur Schopenhauer once posited, "the world in which a man [sic] lives shapes itself chiefly by the way in which he looks at it." Our values and beliefs shape the kinds of experiences, for example, we want young children to have in classrooms. They also affect what adults do in schools and define role relationships among members of a school. If our attitudes about how best to organize large groups of people focus on hierarchical notions of differentiation and classification, then we will tend to conceptualize our supervisory practice as perhaps superior and evaluative. Doing so will negatively affect school climate and send the wrong cultural message for building and sustaining a learning community, which I presume you, my readers, want.

Allow me to close this chapter with a personal case example of how I confronted a rather difficult situation in which I was fortunately able, albeit slowly, to transform a set

> *"Culture is the connective tissue that binds the organization together."*
>
> —Patrick Bernuth

of beliefs and values, in the end resulting in a more healthy and positive school climate. The point here is that what we as principals do plays a very important role in shaping or reshaping culture and building positive school climate.

My first appointment as a school administrator was at "ANYWHERE USA." I arrived at the school last September. My predecessor's reputation was there to greet me.

Mr. Stuart Oswald Blenheim was known as a stickler for every jot, title, and iota inscribed in the Board of Ed's rules and regulations. He carried a tape measure, a portable tape recorder, and a stethoscope and considered teachers to be one of the lower forms of sapient life. The others—in "descending" order—were nonprofessional staff members and students.

This supervisor made his opinions abundantly clear by word and deed. Woe to the pupil caught wandering the halls without appropriate documentation—no excuses accepted. Period. End of message.

Furthermore, the offending miscreant's pedagogue was called on the carpet, raked over the coals, strung up by the thumbs, and subjected to a wide variety of other abusive clichés.

Stuart Oswald was short, so short that it was difficult to see him among a group of eighth or ninth graders. He took full advantage of his camouflage, so that he could spy on his charges. He was known to quietly walk up to a room, place his stethoscope to the door, and gradually straighten his knees and stand on his toes so as to see through the small glass window. Teachers would constantly be on the lookout for a bald head rising in their doors' windows.

Any teacher who observed this latter-day Napoleon lurking in the halls was honor-bound to pass the information on to his or her neighbors. A note referring to "Pearl Harbor," "Incoming Scud Missiles," "Sneak Attack," or "Raid's Here" was enough to raise blood pressure and churn digestive juices.

Last spring, he was appointed as principal in a school on the other side of the city.

Such was Blenheim's repute that all the teachers whom I supervised avoided my presence like the very plague. On one occasion, I passed by a room and noticed a teacher showing great care in assisting a pupil at her desk. Suddenly, the teacher "felt" my presence, quickly straightened her posture, and proceeded nervously to the front of the room to resume writing on the board. I walked away bewildered. However, after ascertaining that I did not suffer from halitosis, dandruff, or terminal body odor, I realized the problem. Honestly, I couldn't blame them. After all, Blenheim's initials suited him perfectly.

Thus, I was forced to overcome this burden and, somehow, to win my teachers' and students' trust.

During my first meeting with my teachers, I asked, rather than told, them not to think of me as their supervisor. I hoped that they would consider me a colleague with perhaps more experience and responsibility in certain areas. I wanted to share my knowledge with them. I wanted to work with them, help them, assist, guide, coach, collaborate . . . I was not going to spy on them. I was not going to humiliate them. I was a real human being, just like they were, just like the children were.

They had a difficult time accepting this. They had been abused for 7 years by a petty tyrant and did not believe that any supervisor could think differently. After all, Blenheim had been rewarded for his fine methods.

I promised that there would be no sneak attacks. We would do our best to cooperate and coexist. I would help them teach more effectively, share my experiences, and readily accept their expertise and ideas.

It took 3 to 6 months of hard work on my part and caution on theirs, but we've finally reached the point where we smile at each other when we meet in the hall. Several of them have come to me with professional and personal problems. They were a bit surprised at some of my proposed solutions. The word got around that Blenheim was really gone.

C H A P T E R   T H R E E

Best Practices in Visionary Leadership

"Embarking upon a career in educational leadership requires both a strong sense of purpose and a clear vision if we are to initiate necessary reforms and to help create the magnificent schools our students so richly deserve."

—Patricia Andersen, leadership
candidate in New York City

Vision both creates and reflects school culture and sets the tone for school climate. As principal, you are expected to articulate a vision that reflects and extends the rich traditions of your institution. Visionary statements are forward looking, yet grounded in the realities of the school in which you work. Without vision, there is no direction or hope for the future. You are responsible for articulating and realizing a compelling vision for the future. Visionary leaders express a pressing need to better define the school's priorities and target resources in support of these priorities. Vision intends to both solidify and reinforce school culture. As principal, you embrace a clear vision of the future that distinguishes your school's personnel, programs, and services.

What is the connection among vision, values (culture), and a sense of mission? A vision usually represents a concise statement of affirmation or purpose that reflects core values of the institution (although it can be used to create new values as well). A mission is a somewhat more detailed description of how to actualize the vision. See the sample below of a fictitious school.

VISION

We at Cramford High School strive for quality and excellence in every facet of our educational program. We are committed to nurturing caring, curious, competent, committed, community-active students who are concerned, above all else, with transforming their own lives and the lives of others.

CORE VALUES

- Respect for the dignity of all persons
- Emphasis on an ethic of caring
- Belief in the power of education to transform lives
- Dedication to service learning
- Affirmation of social justice, equity, and educational opportunity for everyone
- Commitment to appreciating and celebrating diversity and cultural understanding among all people in a free, democratic society
- Belief in education as an empowering ideal
- Commitment to lifelong learning and ethical behavior
- Dedication to making a difference in the academic and social lives of students

MISSION

The mission of Cramford High School is to prepare caring, curious, competent, committed, and community-active students who:

- Demonstrate a strong foundation in their academic disciplines that affords students the skills and intellectual knowledge base upon which mature and in-depth study can be undertaken
- Value experiential learning and interdisciplinary study

- Possess an unwavering respect for learning, diversity, cultural difference, and multicultural education
- Personify an ethic of caring
- Uphold the ideals of justice, equity, and opportunity for all people
- Think creatively, reflectively, and critically in grappling with a panoply of educational challenges
- Maintain high standards of excellence for themselves and for others
- Honor critical lifelong learning

Reflective Questions

1. Assess the value of Cramford's vision, core values, and mission.

2. Describe how you might frame similar ideas in your school. If you have already framed a vision, articulated core values, and published a mission statement, assess the extent to which they are meaningful and useful in your everyday work as school leader.

Successful cultural leaders are able to articulate a vision that inspires others to action. In the pages that follow, you'll be challenged to construct a personal vision platform or lengthy statement that will serve to guide your practice as a visionary principal. The boxed material below summarizes the ideas about visionary leadership that should serve as checkpoints for your own progress as a cultural leader:

What You Should Know About Visionary Leadership

- **Examining Beliefs and Values**—Articulating your beliefs and values is essential in order to frame a vision that is genuine and that can serve to inspire others to success.
- **Composing a Vision Statement**—Vision is developed by asking yourself some key questions that seek to uncover deep-seated beliefs and values.
- **Actualizing Your Vision**—Espousing a vision is not enough; you must put it into practice.

1. EXAMINING BELIEFS AND VALUES

Vision is not developed in isolation of deep-seated personal beliefs and values. Once affirmed and developed, your values are then matched to the context in which you work. For instance, if you fervently support inclusive teaching practices, then you could genuinely articulate a vision for a school founded on inclusion and differentiated learning. The first essential step to visionary leadership is to uncover your beliefs and values.

Reflective Questions

1. What do you really care about most?

2. What do you passionately believe?

3. Is there some issue that you would consider yourself to be uncompromising about? Explain.

4. Based on answers to the preceding questions, what factors, incidents, or people have influenced you the most?

5. How have they contributed to forming your beliefs and values about education and leadership? Explain in detail.

6. Why is uncovering these influences important for better understanding what you believe in?

Our experiences influence us greatly. As B. F. Skinner (1976) posited, social experiences are powerful influences on human behavior. For example, when Mary Johnson is teased by her classmates because of her dress, speech, or possibly awkward behavior, such interactions may negatively affect her self-image. Mocking and criticisms both at home and school may create feelings of inadequacy and increased dependency on others for social and personal acceptance. These social experiences affect how Mary thinks about herself, how she talks about herself, and

> "Culturally proficient leaders first develop a vision and then a mission that serves the needs of all students."
>
> —Randall B. Lindsey, Kikanza Nuri Robbins, and Raymond D. Terrell

how she acts in social situations (e.g., as a social isolate). Similarly, if you were robbed or cheated by someone of a particular ethnic group, then this experience (especially if reinforced by societal stereotypes and possibly reinforced by other people's experiences) may influence the way you think, speak, and act toward someone else from that particular group. The personal experiences we encounter (events that occur in private) also shape our perceptions of reality, our beliefs, and what we value.

We as educational leaders, as all human beings, are influenced by our social and personal experiences as well. Consider these questions:

Reflective Questions

1. How have your experiences influenced your beliefs and values?

2. How have your experiences influenced your behavior on a daily basis?

3. How have your experiences influenced your leadership style?

Other factors also influence our beliefs and values:

- *Familial*—There is no doubt that one's family influences behavior patterns and actions. Aside from the psychological implications of familial influence, such experiences play an enormous role in shaping beliefs and attitudes of children and adolescents. The long-lasting impact of family has also been well documented (e.g., Evans, 2004).

- *Educational*—Educational experiences (influences of educators and programs) are a significant factor in shaping one's philosophic outlook and behavior, especially as these relate to the work experience. Early educational influences clearly have an impact on human behavior (Evans, 2004). Even educational experiences that occur later in life have a substantial influence. For instance, someone trained in clinical supervision is likely to view teacher development differently than someone trained in more traditional supervisory methods.

- *Religious*—Although studies indicate recent decreases of religion in shaping and sustaining behavior (e.g., Neusner, 2003), religion still plays an important role in affecting many individuals (e.g., Harris, 2004).

- *Societal*—Societal influences comprise six concepts:

  History—Historical trends, whether societal or otherwise, shape human behavior and practice (e.g., Bryson, 2003). For example, a historical event such as 9/11 may have reshaped or reframed our view of the importance of making a difference in the lives if children through education.

  Economic—The role of economics in influencing human behavior has been documented (e.g., Sowell, 2002). For example, an economic event such as a stock market crash may affect our lives in significant ways.

  Cultural—Cultural influences are well researched (e.g., Sowell, 1996). For example, the type of music we enjoy may influence our beliefs and attitudes (Judy Collins's and Arlo Guthrie's music, for instance, during the Vietnam War years influenced my antiwar sentiments and other feelings toward education and life).

  Political—The role of politics in shaping human behavior has been explored (e.g., Sowell, 2002). For example, a political event such as a presidential election may affect our ability to earn a living or receive a particular social benefit.

  Social—The dynamics of human relationships, individually or collectively, has also been examined (e.g., Dunn, 1995). For example, our everyday social contacts with people we work with may influence our own beliefs and attitudes. Think of how teenagers may be influenced by their peers (adults, too).

  Ideas—The influence of ideology on our behavior is significant (e.g., Weiss, 1997). For example, the idea that a group of people is intellectually inferior to another based upon skin pigmentation has influenced many people's thoughts and actions toward others.

Reflective Questions

1. How have your family values or experiences influenced you?

2. How have your educational experiences influenced you?

3. How have your religious beliefs influenced you? Can you provide an example of how these beliefs influence a particular stance you take to an educational issue?

4. How has society influenced you? Think, for instance, of how the economic climate, political milieu, or cultural conditions have played a factor in shaping your beliefs.

5. Which environmental influence has played the greatest role in shaping what you believe in?

6. How have your own schooling experiences shaped your current view of best practices in schools?

7. How have any of these concepts or combinations of them influenced your leadership style?

The questions above should help you frame or deepen your personal vision for leadership.

Reflective Question

1. How might these questions help you develop and understand your personal vision for leadership? (Share ideas with a colleague before you read on.)

Consider your responses to all the preceding Reflective Questions. Perhaps you realize that a plethora of factors have "shaped" (or, if you prefer, in non-Skinnerian language, "influenced" or "affected") who you are, what you believe in, and what you care about or value. What are these factors, and how have they influenced you?

Reflective Activities

1. Take pen and paper to hand and record your in-depth response to the previous question. (This activity may take some time; don't rush.)

2. Pair off with a colleague and share with each other the personal factor that has influenced you the most. Explain why. The person listening will report out to the larger group, describing the factor that has influenced the other person.

These reflective activities are meant to help you examine possible factors or influences on the lens you use to perceive the world around you, which in turn influences your beliefs, values, and mission or vision. This vision is critical in determining how you think, speak, and act. Ultimately, such a vision will play an essential role in improving practice and will help you "gain control over" your "own behaviors in the work setting" (Osterman & Kottkamp, 1993, p. 85).

Using these preceding questions or activities as a base, answer the following Reflective Questions, which pertain more specifically to developing a personal vision statement for building and sustaining leadership:

Reflective Questions

1. What are your beliefs and values about learning and the learning capacity of students?

2. What are your beliefs and values about teaching and its impact on student learning?

3. What are your beliefs and values about supervision?

4. What are your beliefs and values about leadership and its role in building and sustaining learning communities?

5. What are your beliefs and values about building and sustaining learning communities?

---

2. COMPOSING A VISION STATEMENT

Having briefly explored a wide array of factors or influences for your espoused beliefs, we now need to articulate them precisely in the form of a position or vision statement related more specifically to leadership. By thinking and writing about your values, you will be on your way to developing and continuously refining a vision statement to guide your practice as a leader.

Follow these general guidelines:

1. Review your responses to the questions previously posed in section 1, "Examining Beliefs and Values."

2. Ask yourself how these responses may relate to your role as a leader.

3. How can they influence your vision statement?

4. Think and reflect upon your philosophy of education, view of teaching and learning, conception of curriculum and supervision, experiences in school, and preferred leadership style.

5. Above all else, as you write this statement, ask yourself, "How can this statement serve to support my personal learning and leadership style as I work to build and sustain a learning community?" (see Sullivan & Glanz, 2006, for more details).

MY STATEMENT

_____

_____

_____

_____

_____

_____

Reflective Questions

1. Reread what you have written. Feel free to rewrite and revise. Is what you have written an accurate reflection of your espoused beliefs for practicing leadership? How do you know for sure?

2. Try to locate two other colleagues and share your statement with them. How do they react to what you have written? Are your statements similar to theirs? Explain. Revise your statement based on feedback received.

3. Revise your vision statement by reviewing the following guiding questions:
   • What has influenced your vision of leadership?
   • What are your goals or hopes for your students?
   • What are the types of skills, attitudes, and feelings you want students to possess?
   • What type of climate is needed to support the student outcomes you identified in your statement?
   • What can you do to help establish that climate?
   • What are your views about teaching and learning?
   • How should instruction be organized and delivered to support the type of climate and student outcomes you desire?
   • How would you promote a positive school culture by providing an effective instructional program, applying best practice to student learning, and designing comprehensive professional growth plans for staff?
   • What is your philosophy on leadership?
   • What can leaders do to create effective schools?
   • How will you exercise leadership in your building?
   • How would you facilitate the development, articulation, implementation, and stewardship of a school vision of learning supported by the school community?
   • Provide examples of how you would act with integrity, fairly, and in an ethical manner.
   • What will the governance structure look like?
   • How would you manage the organization, operations, and resources in a way that promotes a safe, efficient, and effective learning environment?
   • What are your responsibilities as a leader?

- What are your ideas for collaborating with all families and other community members, responding to diverse community interests and needs, and mobilizing community resources?
- How would you seek to understand, respond to, and influence the larger political, social, economic, legal, and cultural context?

For more detailed descriptions on how to develop a vision, see Sullivan and Glanz (2006).

Sample Statement

Janice Micali, a leadership candidate in New York City, offered to share her vision statement:

"There is no more prodigious challenge than that of educating children. Those of us who chose to become educators understand the awesome responsibility that comes with the task. . . . It is our job to ensure that the children of this country and our school master the skills that will enable them to become functioning members of society. . . .

"My vision will be to invite and encourage others to participate in determining and developing my vision into a shared vision that is clear, compelling, and connected to teaching and learning. . . . This vision should clearly create and sustain an environment where all students learn at the highest levels. With this vision, I hope to provide an inspiring image of the future for myself, the staff, the parents, the community, and most importantly, the students.

"A common thread throughout this platform is that education is a process that has an end within itself: the quest for knowledge and understanding. . . . The components of a school culture that reflect my vision are: instructional climate, teaching and learning, student outcomes, and leadership and governance. To understand my vision of leadership, it is necessary to define each component and demonstrate how each is integrated into the school culture while keeping in mind that our school's goal is to aim for excellence in academic achievement, personal development, and social responsibility in a culturally diverse society."

Student Outcomes

"The cornerstone of any educational vision is student outcomes. . . .
The students need to meet rigorous academic standards. The students need
to learn to understand important concepts, develop essential skills, and
apply what they learn to real-world problems. They should value, respect,
and appreciate multiculturalism and diversity. They should become productive and moral citizens, accountable for their learning and actions.
They should be prepared to meet the changing and diverse challenges of a
technological society, therefore becoming technologically literate and
global-minded. The students should be collaborative decision makers,
enthusiastic, confident, and inspired to realize their highest potential. . . .

"My vision supports all students in realizing that they have the
potential to reach high standards. I will encourage the development of
self-discipline, positive self-image, strong personal values, and . . .
respect for all school community members. I will utilize all available
resources, both financial and human, to maximize the effectiveness of
the school and its programs."

Instructional Climate

"The realization of student outcomes is inextricably tied to the
instructional climate. My vision is to truly exemplify that all students
can learn. The students, staff, and parents should feel safe and nurtured.
The school should be seen as a community for learning. All involved are
seen as partners in the education of our children. The school will promote a climate of acceptance and mutual respect. The culture of the
school will support collaboration, foster reflection, and celebrate accom-
plishment. Multiple opportunities for celebration of individual and
schoolwide success in all areas of achievement will be developed.

"It will be a school where everyone is physically and emotionally
safe. It will be a safe, trusting, and collaborative environment that devel-
ops lifelong, self-directed learners. The school will provide a safe and
secure environment where people enjoy learning. It will work in part-
nership with the community. . . .

"The students' work will be displayed throughout the building and
classrooms. Classrooms will be a print- and material-rich environment
that encourages the different learning styles of all children. In order for
the classroom to be an effective learning environment, the teacher
and student must possess joy for learning. The 'arts' will also be
incorporated into the school, so that the students can pursue their

creative sides with music and art. The school will also offer an extensive after-school program that will include sports, tutoring, enrichment, homework help, mommy/daddy and me classes, and the arts.

"The school will also be supported by professional development and workshops. This will allow the staff to have the opportunity to grow, self-assess, reflect, and collaborate. My vision is to support teachers by providing new teacher training, mentor teachers, team teaching, class-room intervisitation, and weekly peer observations in which classrooms will serve as demonstration sites for specific organizational and instruc-tional practices. This will provide a forum for the exchange of ideas, concerns, problems, positive and negative experiences, teaching styles, creativity, and [will] support interaction among the staff. . . .

"My vision will also provide ample opportunity for parents to become involved. There should be active parental involvement in deci-sion making and learning policies. There will be a parent room in the building for parents to receive literature about current issues. It is here that they will be able to speak with the parent coordinator, find/locate extensive resources in multiple languages, read the schedule for upcom-ing parent workshops, and even [find] translators. The parents will be encouraged to get involved with the school as often as possible. They will be viewed as full and equal partners in the educational process and in the daily life of the school."

Teaching and Learning

"The instructional climate is the framework that supports the teaching and learning in the building. Students will have a variety of learning experiences in and outside of the classroom [that] will develop their ability to become lifelong learners. This curriculum will reflect multiple instructional strategies, which will accommodate different needs and learning styles. Students will be grouped heterogeneously according to grade level. I'd like to try to keep class size at a maximum of 20 students for grades K through 2 and 25 for grades 3 through 5.

"Each child will be encouraged to progress at his [or] her own developmental level and speed. Each child's curiosity and creativity will be nurtured. In order to achieve an environment conducive to learning, the teacher must expect appropriate behavior fostering respect and con-sideration for oneself and others.

"The assessment model will incorporate a spectrum of tools so as to support a holistic approach to evaluation. Teachers will be required

to keep portfolios on each student. They will accumulate many observational notes, running records, student exhibits, and assessments in these portfolios. Every aspect of the instructional program will focus on the diverse needs of the students; on their academic, social, and personal growth; and on high standards for student achievement. The school community will be committed to maintaining the same high level of expectations for all students, while acknowledging the individual differences among students meeting the standards, and to encouraging and nurturing student enthusiasm for learning.

"Opportunities for enrichment, intervention, and extracurricular activities will be offered throughout and after the school day. After-school activities provide a perfect bridge between the students, parents, and staff to the school and its community. Another way to promote this bridge will be to hold events like talent shows, music concerts (chorus, band, and dance), and sports competitions, which will get parents into the school to watch their children perform and/or compete. . . ."

Leadership and Governance

"Essential to the realization of my educational vision is a model of leadership that supports collaboration and includes and encourages multiple perspectives. My leadership style will be seen as proactive, flexible, and reflective. I will model values, beliefs, and behaviors. Two specific values that will be encouraged and modeled are honesty and integrity. In this model, the principal will be responsible for providing the time and the structure for students, staff, parents, and other school community members to openly participate in some aspects of the governance process.

"I will be committed to a collaborative approach of leadership and sustain a focus on the fundamental belief that student achievement must drive all aspects of the educational process. I will actively work to secure the resources needed to support the instructional process and to develop and sustain a supportive and open relationship with the community. I will share in both the joys of our successes, and in the struggles of our setbacks.

"Leaders should be able to listen to, affirm, and give value to the thoughts and actions of staff members. Therefore, I will offer support and insight by being visible in classrooms and throughout the building. I will work to maintain an atmosphere of cooperation by allowing for my staff to meet and exchange ideas and concerns. Criticism will be constructive, and all in the school community will have input in the decision-making process.

"The school leader will have the responsibility to see that teacher observations in the classroom setting will be geared toward personal growth and will not have the focus on evaluation. Teachers will be expected to meet with leadership in planning conferences and postconferences where they will choose and react to their own plan for growth through the process. . . .

"The schools of the future must be equipped to handle complex problems. I think it is no longer possible for one person, in the form of a principal, to manage all these problems on his [or] her own. It is essential for the principal to create school management teams that help develop new ideas and add twists and turns to existing ideas in order to improve the school. I think that the key to success is the team concept composed of individuals who truly dedicate themselves to their profession and children. . . .

"This vision statement hopes to connect to the powerful dreams and positive values of staff, students, and parents."

3. ACTUALIZING YOUR VISION

Visionary leadership does not exist without putting your ideas into practice. Almost anyone can compose a vision statement, but your success is dependent on the extent to which you're able to make that vision a reality. The following suggestions are culled from best practices by successful principals who have been able to articulate a sound and meaningful vision and at the same time translate that vision into lived practice:

- Meet frequently with all school and community constituents to discuss your articulated vision for the school.

- Solicit their reactions and input. Ask them, for instance, "What needs to be done in order to make this a reality?"

- Form a committee of volunteers to discuss aspects of your vision, and charge them with charting future directions that can serve to transform ideas into actions.

- Challenge teachers, parents, and others to discuss ways they can partake in making the vision a reality.

- Use symbolic leadership. A vision can be reinforced through the use of appropriate symbols or actions. For instance, a special plaque in the main entrance of the school building to commemorate a former graduate who became a successful millionaire in industry might be used as a symbol for current and future students in the school that communicates that "any of you from this urban school environment can make it."

- Use assessment instruments (e.g., questionnaires, interviews, focus groups, action research) to ascertain the degree to which your vision has been actualized.

Reflective Questions

1. What are other ways you might use symbols to articulate your vision?

2. What else might you need to do to actualize your vision?

CONCLUSION

Vision is created from firmly held beliefs and values. Once articulated, they form the basis for visionary leadership. You may see what others cannot. Teachers, for instance, may get caught up in the quagmire of a particular situation. Yet, you are able to envision possibilities for growth and opportunity when others cannot. You share your thoughts and ideas with all constituents continually. In the process of doing so, you gain the confidence of others as they join to affirm and actualize your vision of hope and success. As cultural leaders, you inspire others through the words, ideas, and symbols you use to create a vision for the future. Read the brief vignette below describing one visionary leader:

Gary Khandrius is working at his desk late at night one hot summer evening in anticipation of meeting faculty at the start of the school year. It's now 2:00 a.m., and he labors over revisions of his vision statement that he's been working on for several months. Gary, a newly assigned principal to a middle school, is a visionary. Naturally creative and imaginative, he realizes that his school needs visionary leadership, because the former principal, who was an excellent manager, lacked the ability to inspire the faculty beyond ensuring that they followed district and state curricular guidelines. He knew he wanted to challenge his teachers to excellence by reconfiguring the school by implementing block scheduling and an interdisciplinary approach to curriculum. Utilizing the strengths of the school and its faculty, he knew they could rise to the occasion. He was determined to provide the vision to jump-start them.

He had already begun to share his idea with the school leaders he met over the summer. They were impressed with Gary. One union leader confided to another, "He seems genuine and willing to collaborate. I don't think he'll impose his new ideas, but will rather share his ideas and then engage faculty in an open discussion." "Yes, I agree," said the other teacher-leader. "He has much charisma and vision. He may be the person we need at the right time."

Once the school year began, Gary spoke with teachers, parents, and students at every opportunity he could about his vision. He was able to translate some abstract curricular ideas into an easy-to-understand and practical format, much appreciated by all. Some of the visionary leadership strategies he employed included the following:

1. Spoke at length with the superintendent and her deputy about his ideas and plans for the school

2. Spoke informally with every receptive teacher and parent he saw

3. Formed a volunteer committee to explore block scheduling and interdisciplinary curriculum

4. Had teams of teachers visit "blue ribbon" schools where these ideas were in full use

5. Encouraged revisions and refinements of his ideas, but at the same time expected some sort of implementation plan by the start of the new year

6. Created posters and signs describing and explaining block scheduling and interdisciplinary curriculum

7. Shared professional literature in the areas with faculty and parents

8. Hired a few consultants to introduce the concepts to faculty

9. Continued to engage faculty and community members in actively taking part in the planning process

---

Reflective Questions

1. What other strategies could Gary have used?

2. What factor(s) may have contributed to Gary's ultimate success?

3. What are some of the strengths of such a leader? What do you think may be some weaknesses of such a leader?

4. Draw some conclusions about visionary leadership from the vignette.

5. How would you emulate Gary's actions? What might you do differently?

CHAPTER FOUR

Best Practices in Promoting Cultural Diversity

"Multicultural education is a concept that incorporates cultural differences and provides equality in schools. For it to become a reality in the formal school situation, the total environment must reflect a commitment to multicultural education. The diverse cultural backgrounds and microcultural memberships of students and families are as important in developing effective instructional strategies as are their physical and mental capabilities. Further, educators must understand the influence of racism, sexism, classism on the lives of their students and ensure that these are not perpetuated in the classroom [and in the school]."

—Donna M. Gollnick and Philip C. Chinn

A book devoted to cultural leadership must necessarily discuss the importance of promoting cultural diversity in schools. Support for cultural diversity must start from the top, so to speak. For too long, our educational system has been based on only the rhetoric of equality and justice. Unfortunately, the reality is that there are social, economic, and political conditions that contribute toward, and help to legitimize, inequalities (see, e.g., Apple, 1986; Giroux, 1991; Ogbu, 1978; Spring, 1994). Moreover, public schooling has perpetuated and reinforced social class, racial, and gender stratifications in a number of insidious ways. We as principals must champion opposition to theories and practices that do not support the rights of all individuals to a fair and equal education.

Inequities are clearly evident in each of the following ways: unequal allocations of resources to different schools (Kozol, 1991), socially stratified arrangements for delivering subject matter (Oakes, 1985), low teacher expectations (Rosenthal & Jacobson, 1968), the biased content of curricular materials (Anyon, 1981), patriarchal relations through authority patterns and staffing (Strober & Tyack, 1980), and differential distribution of knowledge by gender within classrooms (M. Sadker & D. Sadker, 1994). One of the most fundamental questions that needs continuous and vigilant attention is "How can we as principals promote the ideals of equality, justice, and opportunity in our classrooms, schools, and communities?"

Gender bias is one striking example of how inequities persist in America's classrooms (M. Sadker & D. Sadker, 1994). What expectations do we form regarding students based on gender? What opportunities are not afforded females that are readily made available to males? Tauber (1997), in *Self-Fulfilling Prophecy: A Practical Guide to Its Use in Education*, presents a list of questions teachers must pose to become aware of how expectations about gender affect students:

Do you assign tasks on some gender basis? Does it just seem natural to assign heavier and dirtier tasks (i.e., carry this, move that) to the "stronger sex" and the more domestic activities (i.e., wash this, clean that, serve this) to the "weaker sex"? When leaders are selected, whether for a classroom or a playground activity, are males more often chosen than females? When creative activities (i.e., decorating for an upcoming holiday) are undertaken, are females more likely than males to be called upon?

When you conduct demonstrations, are males more often asked to assist you and females more often asked to be "recording secretaries"? Do you let female students get away with inappropriate behavior that you would discipline male students for? If you are female, do you catch yourself identifying more with the female students than with the male students? And the list goes on and on. (pp. 47–48)

Communicating positive expectations for all students regardless of gender, age, ethnicity, and social class is a primary professional responsibility of all educators.

As principal, you must recognize the importance of a multicultural education. According to Boyer and Baptiste (1996), multicultural education transforms "education so that its reality for students includes equity for all, a true spirit of democracy, freedom from prejudice and stereotypes of discrimination, and appreciation for cultural diversity" (p. 2).

As educators, we recognize the responsibility of providing all our students with educational opportunities that prepare them to function effectively and productively in a multicultural, multiethnic, multiracial, and global society. To endorse these notions is to understand that diversity is more than "seeing" ethnically diverse people around a table. Perhaps equally important is having people who "think" in diverse ways (Glanz, 1998b).

> "Culturally competent school leaders understand that effective leadership in a diverse environment is about changing the manner in which we work with those who are culturally different from ourselves."
>
> —Randall B. Lindsey, Laraine M. Roberts, and Franklin CampbellJones

Our challenge is certainly to promote cultural diversity on many levels. We need to infuse diversity into our curricula. We need to see and live diversity. Yet, a "school or district should not simply look diverse (ethnically, culturally, or racially), but should be used to lend perspectives and gain the richest information possible on how to best educate both minority and majority-based students as well" (Glickman & Mells, 1997, p. 342). The very foundation of American democracy is inextricably entwined with the attempt to embrace and achieve diversity.

This chapter highlights three important aspects of cultural diversity: encouraging teaching in culturally relevant ways, debunking some myths about culturally relevant pedagogy, and learning to lead keeping culture in mind.

> **What You Should Know About**
> **Promoting Cultural Diversity**
>
> - **Encouraging Culturally Relevant Teaching**—Principals believe supporting cultural diversity benefits all students because of the belief that all students can learn, albeit at different paces and in different ways.
> - **Debunking Myths About Culturally Relevant Pedagogy**—Principals must dispel misconceptions others have about culturally relevant pedagogy.
> - **Leading in Culturally Relevant Ways**—Principals must proactively combat prejudices and take proactive measures to serve as cultural leaders.

1. ENCOURAGING CULTURALLY RELEVANT TEACHING

As principal, you would encourage the views and work of Maria and Mark. Maria Rodriguez is a middle school teacher in an urban Los Angeles school district, and Mark Ramler is a high school teacher in a suburban district in Washington, DC. Both teachers are aware that in almost 20 years about 40% of the nation's school-age children will represent people of color. They also know that schools have not met the educational needs of culturally diverse students very well. Although Maria and Mark come from different cultural backgrounds, they share a common pedagogical approach that emphasizes culturally appropriate and relevant teaching strategies. Mark and Maria are sensitive to and cognizant of the extent to which a student's cultural background may influence learning and attitudes toward school in general. They are responsive to their students by incorporating elements of the students' culture in their teaching.

Culturally responsive teachers (Jordan Irvine & Armento, 2003) make special efforts to get to know their students really well. Mark and Maria ask their students to share stories about their families and cultural heritage. Students are encouraged to express themselves openly about their culture. Students obtain a tremendous sense of pride and a feeling of being appreciated. Maria assigns her students a homework assignment to write a story about their family. Sensitive to the fact that *family* may mean something different to different students, Maria encourages an accepting, warm atmosphere in her class conducive to student participation. She, in fact, shares her own cultural background with students, which serves to ease their apprehensions and encourages them to share as well. Mark realizes that culturally relevant teaching is much more than reviewing the contributions of Dr. Martin Luther King Jr. on his national day of observance. Mark's culturally responsive pedagogy is integrated into his curriculum and

> *"The first factor for principal leadership in improving teaching and learning is understanding the school's culture."*
>
> —L. Joseph Matthews and Gary M. Crow

lessons on almost a daily basis, not just around holidays or special commemorations. He refers to King's work when, for instance, students don't appreciate a policy established by the school administration. He uses their anger as a teaching opportunity to share how Dr. King worked within the system to effect the changes he desired. Then, Mark asks his students, "How might we work with administration to change that policy?" When the issue is brought to students' attention in this way, they are not only receptive but are willing to begin discussions with students and faculty.

Culturally responsive teachers and principals know that students' culture (values, beliefs, and norms) might clash with institutional values, beliefs, and norms. Some students who do not volunteer in class, for example, might be perceived as lazy or learning disabled. Other students are taught not to look into the eyes of an authority figure. Maria once overheard another teacher chastise an Asian girl for not looking at her when she spoke. The teacher said, "I know in your culture you don't look up when spoken to, but you're in America now, look up at me." Culturally aware teachers take into consideration students' cultural norms; in this way, students feel appreciated and respected. Academic success is more likely when teachers are culturally sensitive.

Reflective Questions

1. How might you, as principal, remain culturally sensitive?

2. How might you encourage or ensure that a child's culture is appreciated and respected schoolwide?

Below are some suggestions for paying attention to social and cultural customs culled from Kottler and Kottler (2002, p. 20) in their *Children With Limited English: Teaching Strategies for the Regular Classroom.* Pay attention to the following:

- Verbal communication (pronunciation, patterns of speech, tempo of speech, etc.)
- Nonverbal communication (eye contact, meaning of gestures)
- Proxemics (spatial distance between people)
- Social values (peer group influences)
- Intellectual orientation (e.g., is frequent questioning valued or discouraged?)

As principal, you can do much to encourage culturally relevant teaching by your words and deeds. As cultural leader of the school, you are responsive to different ethnic, linguistic, and religious subcultures, and you realize that various subcultures, for a variety of reasons, might be subject to prejudices and even exclusion from school activities simply because they "appear" different. By valuing diversity and preserving the cultural dignity of your students, you serve as a "culturally proficient school leader" (Lindsey, Roberts, & CampbellJones, 2005). As cultural leader, you affirm justice and opportunity for all students in your school, and you work hard to create an inclusive learning environment that supports and encourages all students to succeed, academically and socially. Your work as principal is guided by five principles that, according to Lindsey et al. (2005), "open up opportunities to build culturally proficient and functionally diverse educational communities in which people interact with one another in respectful and culturally responsive ways" (p. 21). In the end, these five principles support culturally relevant teaching:

- Culture is a predominant force in people's lives.
- People are served in varying degrees by the dominant culture.
- People have both personal identities and group identities.
- Diversity within cultures is vast and significant.
- Each individual and each group has unique cultural value and needs.

2. DEBUNKING MYTHS ABOUT CULTURALLY RELEVANT PEDAGOGY

Cultural leaders actively seek to counter the following myths or misconceptions about culturally relevant pedagogy.

Misperceptions About Culturally Relevant Pedagogy

(Ideas drawn from Jordan Irvine & Armento, 2003, pp. 13, 14)

1. *Misperception: Culturally responsive pedagogy is a new and special pedagogy that is relevant only to low-income, urban students of color.*
    Reality: Traditional pedagogy has always been culturally relevant. Middle-class and European American students' culture is the accepted norm in most schools. Can you list some ways in which middle-class students' culture is acceptable in schools?

_____

_____

_____

_____

_____

_____

_____

2. *Misperception: In schools with diverse students, only teachers of color are capable of demonstrating culturally responsive pedagogy.*
    Reality: Most teachers (and principals) are white. It is unrealistic and undesirable to equate culturally relevant pedagogy only with teachers of color. All teachers, regardless of their ethnic background, are capable of incorporating this kind of pedagogy. All it takes is a sensitivity and an appreciation of its importance. Are you capable of teaching or leading in culturally relevant ways? Explain.

_____

_____

_____

_____

_____

_____

_____

_____

3. *Misperception: Culturally responsive pedagogy is primarily a teaching method.*
    Reality: Yes, it is, but it is much more. Culturally relevant teaching is an attitude about teaching, students, the ways they can learn, and outside factors that influence successful learning. Why are your teachers inclined or not inclined to teach this way? Explain.

_____

_____

_____

_____

_____

_____

4. *Misperception: Culturally relevant educators must become expert in a variety of cultures.*
    Reality: That is not possible, nor is it necessary. All that educators need to know and believe is that culture plays a vital role in terms of understanding student behavior and learning. Do you

really believe that culture makes a difference in student achievement? Explain.

_____

_____

_____

_____

_____

_____

_____

_____

Reflective Questions

1. How can schools appreciate the culture of all students?
2. What factors might mitigate against incorporating culturally relevant pedagogy?
3. What training might you need to lead teachers in culturally relevant pedagogy?

3. LEADING IN CULTURALLY RELEVANT WAYS

Cultural leaders actively lead in culturally relevant ways by incorporating these strategies, among others:

- *Consider the role of race, gender, social class, and sexual orientation.* You realize that race matters, as does gender, sexual orientation, and class. Students' backgrounds, and the way they have been treated by society as a result, influence their behavior. As principal, you raise and discuss the following questions:

1. What ways might teachers overtly or unintentionally discriminate in their classrooms?
2. What ways might schools (principals) overtly or unintentionally discriminate?
3. What are some prejudices educators might have about some people or groups, and how might such prejudices affect these educators' behavior in the classroom?
4. What are some ways teachers might promote equality, opportunity, and justice?
5. What are some ways schools (principals) might promote equality, opportunity, and justice?

- *Take steps to prevent school violence.*

He was a 49-year-old black man living in Jasper, Texas. The three white men (John William King, Shawn Allen Berry, and Lawrence Russell Brewer) charged with his murder chained the man to the back of a pickup truck and dragged him behind the truck until his body came apart. The three men took the body parts and left them near a black cemetery.

He was a gay University of Wyoming student who was found beaten and tied to a fence post on the Wyoming prairie.

He was a Jewish physician who performed abortions in Buffalo, New York. He was shot with a high-powered rifle through his kitchen window in front of his wife and children.

The names of James Byrd, Matthew Shepard, and Barnett Slepian have been echoed in our consciousness ever since their brutal murders several years ago. These horrific murders are poignant reminders that hatred is ever present and, perhaps, endemic to American culture and society.

Have you ever hated someone? I think we all have felt intense anger toward someone. How did we react? Did we shout at them, hit them, or plan revenge, or did we merely conjure up images of retaliation? Occasionally, our passions and tempers get the better of us. We lose control. Yet, you may argue, you would never resort to such extreme acts of hatred as described above. Granted.

What about our tendencies toward bigotry and prejudice? If you are Christian, have you ever harbored ill will toward a Muslim? What about resentment toward Jews? If you are Israeli, have you ever thought badly about Arabs? What about intolerance and hate between Indians and Pakistanis, Asians and Westerners, Swedes and Norwegians, Hispanics and whites, whites and African Americans, and Serbs and Kosovars?

Why is it that our fear, suspicion, and hatred of others different from us have overpowered our good sense and moral commitments to civility, good will, justice, and tolerance? When we think of Columbine, Colorado, we now know that the kids who committed the murders had been bullied. School violence is on the rise, and we as educators must consider the way students treat others who are different.

As principal, you might engage in these activities, among others:

1. Create forums for open discussions about cultural diversity during faculty meetings, grade conferences, parent-teacher meetings, and so forth.
2. Invite keynote speakers on various aspects of cultural diversity for students, teachers, parents, and community.
3. Encourage development of multicultural fairs.
4. Examine curriculum to incorporate cultural diversity projects on a consistent basis.
5. Form committees of students, parents, and teachers to discuss school violence and to identify key problem areas in the school.
6. Listen, listen, and listen some more to what students are experiencing and saying.
7. Affirm and demand sound, positive values of tolerance and mutual respect for all people.
8. When a problem occurs, nip it in the bud.

- *Focus on fundamental instructional issues.* Although you are cognizant of the many political complexities that affect a school or district, focus on what really matters to students— instruction. Strive to encourage good pedagogy and teaching. Faculty and grade meetings should focus almost exclusively on instructional issues. Build a culture that supports instruction.

- *Understand that the "means" are even more important than the "end."* Certainly, some people will judge you only by your results. However important results are, you must realize that how you go about accomplishing them demonstrates your level of integrity. Raising test scores, for instance, is important only to the extent that students are engaged in meaningful learning activities and that teachers are providing instructionally and culturally sound pedagogy.

- *Realize your context expertise.* As a cultural leader, you have the capacity to understand and work well in multiple contexts (urban, suburban, multicultural, and global). You also should realize your ability to develop positive interactions in multiple communities (families, communities, and agencies). Continue to demonstrate a commitment to specific knowledge, understanding, and skills needed for relating to and taking account of these contexts. Also, appreciate all aspects of cultural diversity among students and community.

- *Examine your own biases.* The word *prejudice*, derived from the Latin noun *praejudicium*, originally meant precedent—a judgment based on previous decisions and experiences. Later, the word came to mean a judgment formed before examining and considering all the facts. It is not easy to say how much fact is required in order to justify a judgment. A prejudiced person will say she or he has sufficiently considered all the facts to warrant a viewpoint. She or he may then relate all the negative experiences she or he has had with Catholics, Jews, Irish, Hispanics, and so on. Examining one's biases presupposes the understanding that everyone is prejudiced to some degree; that is, everyone sometimes makes prejudgments about people and in situations. "Are all or most women poor drivers?" "Do all or most Asians excel in math and science?" "Are all or most Jews interested in making money?" "Are all or most African Americans low achievers?" What are your prejudices? How do you know? What do you do to ensure that they don't affect your decisions as an educational leader?

- *Take action to combat bias.* Taking *action* to combat oppression is an important responsibility of a cultural leader. What action have you recently taken to demonstrate your commitment to combating bias? Check off which of the following statements describe you presently:

_____ I tell or listen to jokes that aim to put people down.

_____ I believe that most people in schools are not oppressed in any way.

_____ I am aware that oppression exists, but I don't know what to do about it.

_____ I read books or attend workshops and seminars to learn more about these issues.

_____ I actively support others who speak out or take action against oppression.

_____ I consciously work to change individual and institutional actions and policies that discriminate against others. I also plan educational programs to combat bias and hate.

• *Confront curricular bias.* Although textbooks over the past 10 years have improved in terms of ensuring nonracist and nonsexist books, problems still persist. Consider these seven forms of bias that may exist in various instructional materials (see, e.g., Zittleman & Sadker, n.d.):

Invisibility: Do the materials, for example, omit African Americans, Latinos, and Asian Americans?

Stereotyping: Do the materials, for example, portray only men and boys?

Imbalance and Selectivity: Do the materials, for example, make reference only to European discoveries regarding math and science?

Unreality: Do the materials, for example, gloss over unpleasant facts and events in history, such as the degree to which a genocide was committed against Native Americans?

Fragmentation and Isolation: Do the materials, for example, present information in a fragmented way, such as providing an isolated box separate from the main textual materials entitled "Ten Black Achievers in Science"?

Linguistic Bias: Do the materials, for example, describe non-English speakers as "alien"?

Cosmetic Bias: Do the materials, for example, suggest that the materials are bias free by displaying a cover that is multicultural whereas the narrative in the text is exclusionary?

Form a committee of students, teachers, and parents to examine instructional materials to identify these seven forms of curricular bias. Then (always taking an action) develop ways to remove these biases.

- *Promote multicultural education.* Examine your school through a multicultural lens. Multicultural education consists of five dimensions (Banks, 1997): content integration (e.g., the degree to which teachers use examples from a variety of cultures), equity pedagogy (e.g., teaching that facilitates achievement for all students), empowering school culture and structure (e.g., practices that avoid labeling), prejudice reduction (e.g., activities that promote positive interactions with those different from oneself), and knowledge construction (e.g., examining who determines what gets taught).

- *Demonstrate through your actions that people come first.* I'll never forget the time when I was a teacher and our car pool was stuck in a massive traffic jam on one of the major thoroughfares in the city. The entire office knew about the traffic jam, because the office secretaries always had the radio on in the office in the morning. We eventually arrived, although we were 45 minutes late. Although the principal knew the reason we were late, he charged, "How dare you be so unprofessional!" I tried to explain our situation, but to no avail. He retorted, "You should have had alternate means of transportation." He abruptly left the room, and we, dismayed and shell-shocked, proceeded to our classrooms. This principal clearly did not empathize with us. According to his view, we should have anticipated the traffic and left home 1 hour earlier, as he had done. Right or wrong, his treatment of us that morning was upsetting, lamentable, and unforgettable. How have you recently demonstrated that people come first?

- *Communicate an "ethic of caring."* Improve your listening skills. The next time a staff member has experienced a personal challenge, ask her or him about what happened. Listen, say you're sorry, and offer to help in any way. That's it; that's all you should or could do. Also, inspire all those you meet to aspire to excellence. Offer them the means to do so by providing appropriate resources and suggestions, if they inquire.

- *Examine the following works for other ideas:* Lindsey, Robins, and Terrell (2003) and Lindsey et al. (2005).

Reflective Question

1. What other proactive measures do you use to lead in culturally relevant ways?

CONCLUSION

Providing cultural leadership by focusing on best practices for promoting cultural diversity is a moral imperative. Each of us entered education, and administration in particular, to make a difference in the lives of students. We see the uniqueness of each child, of each person, and try our utmost to light that spark of potential that lies dormant within. We realize that our task also is not just to help our students do well in school but, more important, to succeed in life. We encourage children by teaching them to be caring, moral, and productive members of society. We treat teachers with respect and dignity and as professional in their own right. Noddings (1992) makes the point, "We should educate all . . . not only for competence but also for caring. Our aim should be to encourage the growth of competent, caring, loving, and lovable people" (p. xiv). Cultural diversity study provides a forum to sensitize students and others to the nature of prejudice, intolerance, discrimination, and worse. . . . I am fond of paraphrasing Samuel Totten (Totten & Feinberg, 2000), who said that education may not put an end to prejudice, discrimination, hatred, and terrorism, but it can serve as an instrument to raise the consciousness of people in terms of what it means to be a just and caring individual in a world rife with indifference, injustices, and brutality. Addressing issues of cultural diversity; championing the rights of all people; and leading for equality, justice, and opportunity are at the essence of cultural leadership.

CHAPTER FIVE

Best Practices in Fostering Organization Self-Renewal

"The self-renewing school possesses three essential characteristics: First, a culture that supports adaptability and responsiveness to change. . . . Second, a set of clear-cut, explicit, and well-known procedures through which participants can engage in . . . collaborative problem-solving. Third, . . . a school that knows when and how to reach out to seek appropriate ideas and resources for use in solving its problems."

—Robert C. Owens

"Life is about growth, . . . and growth is about dealing with change."

—Rudolph Giuliani

S chool culture and climate must be viewed within the context of the school as an organization. Many definitions of organizations abound (Green, 2005). Theories of school administration including Taylor's scientific management, Fayol's administrative management, and Weber's bureaucracy represent classical organizational theories that rely on fixed guidelines or hierarchical control of individual work to ensure compliance to rules and regulations; such systems aim for efficiency above all else (Owens, 2004). Human relations theory, with the work of Elton Mayo, Kurt Lewin, and Jacob Moreno, among others, presented a sharp contrast to classical theorists by focusing more on individual initiative and democratic, not bureaucratic, processes for work (Sergiovanni & Starratt, 1997). A set of ideas that tried to find some balance between classical and human relations perspectives was garnered from the behavioral sciences. The work of Chris Argyris, Jacob Getzels and Egon Guba, Abraham Maslow, Douglas McGregor, Frederick Herzberg, and Fred Fiedler, among many others, attempted to reconcile the role of individuals with the needs of the organization (Owens, 2004). This latter body of work contributed enormously to viewing organizational behavior in complex ways.

Another useful approach to understanding human behavior within the school organization has been the study of Social Systems Theory. According to Green (2005), this theory "provides a way of viewing the organization as a whole, taking into consideration the interrelationships among its parts and its interaction with its internal and external environments" (p. 53). Figure 5.1 is an attempt to view the school organization from an open systems perspective. Schools do not operate in isolation of external influences. External forces affect teaching and learning (e.g., the No Child Left Behind Act of 2001 has transformed the way we approach schooling in the United States today), as they also influence the very structure of the school. Although these external influences play an important role in shaping what goes on in schools, several key internal processes are equally important to consider. Student achievement, for example, is influenced greatly by the nature and quality of school leadership, the principal playing no mean role here. Also critical is the school context (e.g., internal and external community groups, whose vested interests

Figure 5.1   External and Internal Influences on School as an
Organization

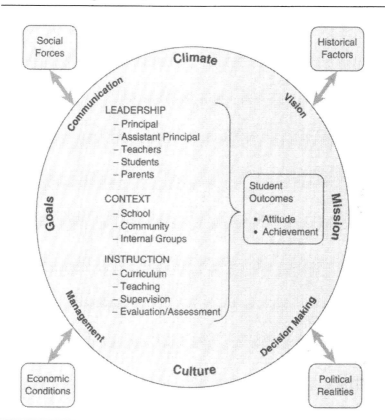

influence what gets taught and how). Obviously, the instructional
process (i.e., curriculum, teaching, and supervision) must receive
primary attention. Leadership, context, and instruction influence
each other and should not be viewed as separate processes within
the school organization. They are influenced by, but also influence, school vision, goals, and mission; the way the school is managed; how communication occurs; and how decisions are made.
School culture and climate (both classroom and organizational)
play significant roles, as we described in Chapter 2.

Schools as open social systems, although dynamic and complex, are subject to many external and internal problems. Often

subject to the vicissitudes of forces beyond its control, the school as an organization and the individuals who work within the school must remain flexible, willing, and able to alter course to adapt to change but must at the same time remain grounded in the school's ultimate mission (i.e., promoting student growth, achievement, and otherwise). Schools cannot stagnate and remain unresponsive to positive and necessary change. When they do, they are highly susceptible to serious problems, such as low teacher morale, intergroup conflict, parental discontent, and low levels of student achievement. Schools must respond affirmatively to change. A school, as a dynamic, open social system, must utilize its internal and external resources to self-renew. Principals who understand the dynamic and complex nature of the school as organization are in an optimal position to marshal external and internal forces so that a renewed sense of mission and purpose is achieved. Sensitive to these forces, you as principal can reshape school culture and effect a positive organizational climate through a renewed sense of vision and mission by opening channels for communication, encouraging participatory management practices including shared decision making, reducing negative conflict, and promoting instructional excellence at all levels. The remainder of this chapter provides strategies and suggestions for renewing our schools.

What You Should Know About Promoting Cultural Diversity

- **Dealing With the Problem of Change**—Principals should understand the opportunities that change can bring. As someone once posited (I paraphrase), change can occur without improvement, but no improvement can occur without change.
- **Dealing With the Problem of Conflict**—Principals realize that conflict is inevitable. Strategies for enhancing communication go a long way toward reducing potentially harmful conflicts.
- **Dealing With the Challenge of Renewal**—Principals are forward looking and always look for ways to improve their organization. Strategies for school renewal are as crucial today as ever.

1. DEALING WITH THE PROBLEM OF CHANGE

Ever since the publication of *The One Minute Manager* (Blanchard & Johnson, 1983) and *Who Moved My Cheese?* (Johnson & Blanchard, 1998), the notion of dealing with change has been in the forefront of the public arena. Of course, those of us in education were always very aware of the nature of change, because we've been subjected to a plethora of reform initiatives since the late 19th century (Ravitch, 1995). However, dealing with these changes effectively is quite another matter (Sarason, 1996).

Although many strategies for dealing with change abound, I have always found the literature on paradigm shifting intriguing and useful (Glanz & Behar-Horenstein, 2000). Simply explained, a *paradigm* is a perspective or lens through which we view a situation; it's the way each of us sees the world or the school organization. Paradigms are the rules we use to perceive reality. Indeed, they help us filter reality. Paradigms are made up of a set of assumptions. If incoming data don't fit with our paradigm, we will likely not perceive and accept them. Using the example of the school as an organization, if we see bureaucracy as the primary way to structure schools, then we are unlikely to foster individual initiative or democratic practices.

The following are some ideas to keep in mind regarding paradigms:

- They are common and normal.
- They are useful; they help us solve problems.
- They can be limiting.

This latter problem is very much related to our discussion of change in this chapter. If we stubbornly hold on to a paradigm that is either incorrect (e.g., the world is flat, women have no right to vote, or learning means listening to the teacher; see Conclusion for more educationally related examples) or out of date, at best (e.g., viewing parents as outsiders, not partners, or seeing ability grouping, not inclusion, as being in the best interests of all students), then we will be unwilling to see other possibilities or reasons to change. Educators, particularly principals, must break out of what has been termed *paradigm paralysis*, that is, the belief that there is only one way of doing things and that there is no other or better way. Therefore, paradigm shifting is so necessary. Our ability to develop multiple paradigms or perspectives is crucial for our success as cultural leaders.

How then can we avert paradigm paralysis?

• *Be open to new ideas.* This suggestion seems so obvious. It's easy if your old paradigm isn't working (e.g., student achievement levels keep dropping). It's more difficult, though, if your old paradigm is somewhat successful. Ask yourself these questions: (a) How do I know it's successful? (b) What kind of success are we talking about? (c) Is one area successful but another less so? and (d) Is it possible something else might be more successful? Reflective practice here is so critical. Visiting other school systems can open us to new ways of doing things. Listening to and hearing what teachers, parents, and students have to say is necessary.

• *Frame realistic goals for change.* You are always ready to conceive and implement change efforts aimed at improving schools and classrooms. However, others may not share your eagerness for the changes you advocate. Establish practical instructional and curricular goals. Also, attend to the next important idea.

• *Seek supporters or allies.* Change is not likely to occur unless you identify reliable change agents who are like-minded and positioned to implement change.

• *Realize that neither centralization nor decentralization works.* Both top-down and bottom-up strategies are necessary to effect district or school change (Fullan, 1997). Use your talents to facilitate both processes.

• *As change agent, you are a designer, not a crusader.* Work as a leader to design learning processes whereby people are mentored, coached, and helped along the way. Older conceptions of school leadership stress decision-making and problem-solving skills as paramount. Although these are important, you are first and foremost a facilitator of change.

- *Build allies.* Resistance to change is strong. Lead by example; don't "go it alone." Learn to build alliances through consensus building in order to support initiatives and programs. Such practices will result in greater school-based implementation.

- *Learn to tolerate chaos and at times to "go with the flow."* Although you may prefer an orderly, predictable work environment, you should realize the value of "organized chaos." Confusion and uncertainty inspire some individuals to learn better. Realize that some people work better in chaotic environments. Also, appreciate the fact that you cannot control everything. To attempt to do so will only increase levels of anxiety and stress. Come to understand emotionally that there is no way to control the world, but you can have control over yourself and the way you react to events.

Reflective Questions

1. Do you avoid change? Do you see change as potentially good for your organization? Explain your views using concrete experiences to support your position.

2. If you don't handle change well, what strategies have you learned to help you think about change differently?

---

2. DEALING WITH THE PROBLEM OF CONFLICT

Some of us try to avoid conflict at all costs. We feel more secure in a state of equilibrium. We simply don't want to "rock the boat." "After all," one of my colleagues confided, "why make things difficult?" First of all, working in a place called "school" is anything but tranquil and uncomplicated. Equilibrium is impossible to achieve for any

> *"Vitality springs from experienc[ing] conflict and tension in systems which also incorporate anxiety-containing supportive relationships. Collaborative cultures are innovative not just because they recognize the value of dissonance inside and outside the organization."*
>
> —Michael Fullan

sustained period of time. Nor is equilibrium something we should seek. We work in a dynamic, ever-changing environment and one in which conflict of some sort is inevitable, if not desirable.

We should view conflict as natural, not to be avoided, and even beneficial, if constructive. The words of Uline, Tschannen-Moran, and Perez (2004) are instructive:

Conflict is present within our schools whether we like it or not. Too often educators feel they must present a united front in the face of students who challenge adult authority, administrators who challenge faculty authority, and the larger community already quick to question the school's institutional authority. Even those teachers and administrators who seek to change traditional norms of practice may be inclined to extend unconditional support rather than to challenge one another, yet again. Educators must find ways to legitimize critique and controversy within organizational life. The rules of courtesy and civility do not necessarily run counter to criticism. It is important to find ways to maintain the former without silencing the latter. Controversy can assume a valued and accepted role in the life of schools. (p. 813)

Uline et al. claim that

Conflict is a natural part of collective human experiences. In our efforts to cooperate with one another, we have differences of opinion about how best to accomplish our common goals. . . . Most conflict is unsettling. . . . It leaves us ill at ease, so we [tend] to avoid or suppress it. . . . Yet these differences . . . have the capacity to inform, perhaps advance, our collective efforts. Each might provide a provocative stimulus, moving us to think more deeply and, ultimately, to act more prudently. Thus, conflict becomes a necessary locus of energy, rather than a source of harm. (p. 782)

Moreover, Uline et al. assert that "avoidance of conflict can leave a persistent undercurrent of tension that saps the organization's energy and enthusiasm" (p. 783).

So the question for us is, can we find ways to constructively deal with conflict?

> **Reflective Question**
>
> 1. You don't need examples of conflict; you likely experience conflicts weekly, if not daily. How, then, do you deal with conflict?

As a cultural leader, you continually nurture shared beliefs and values. Attempting to get others to contribute to common vision or shared anything is frustrating and difficult at times. Therefore, as a cultural leader you must learn to effectively confront conflict in positive ways in order to build a strong culture and a healthy organizational environment. Here are some research-based strategies, among others, for constructively dealing with conflict.

- *Accept, even embrace conflict.* It's inevitable; don't be frightened of conflict. See it as a symptom of something awry in the organization. Use it as an opportunity for reflection, action, and growth.

- *Provide structural organizational policies and cultural practices to encourage constructive controversy.*

1. Communication sessions—Conduct very brief communication briefings via e-mail, loudspeaker announcements, newsletters, and face-to-face meetings (formal and informal).

2. Critical friends groups—Getting together teachers on a grade level, for instance, and encouraging them to use one another to share ideas and then critique their ideas in an atmosphere of trust and cooperation goes a long way to fostering goodwill. Disagreements are articulated and discussed. Although resolutions may not come at first, continued dialogue will clarify positions and help the group to reach consensus or, if consensus proves impossible, to agree to disagree.

3. Training in productive argumentation—Uline et al. (2004) explain,

   teachers might better realize the power of the very experiences they themselves structured for their students through academic exhibitions and senior thesis defenses.

In following the [tenets] of rational deliberation, that is, generating ideas, collecting relevant information, structuring logical arguments, advancing tentative solutions based on current understandings, and keeping an open mind to alternative perspectives, teachers would begin to build confidence in their ability to "use conflict to understand opposing positions, develop alternatives, and integrate apparently disparate positions." (p. 812)

- *Improve communication skills.* Sharpening the interpersonal skills that are based on listening and communication is a key step that will minimize negative conflicts. As principal, you could engage faculty and staff in professional development sessions that seek to teach communication techniques and to understand barriers to communication. Use the script described below.

Communication Techniques

Awareness of how carefully we listen is the first step in improving our listening skills. The next step is to acquire techniques that will facilitate effective listening. Half of the battle is your ability to focus on the speaker; the other half is to communicate to the speaker that you are listening carefully and to verify that you have understood what the speaker is trying to express or convey.

The three types of techniques that follow promote effective listening and understanding (see also Table 5.1). The techniques in the first category, listening techniques, have a dual purpose: They encourage the speaker to continue and indicate that you are following carefully; they support your listening by inserting brief comments that relate to the content of the message. The techniques in the second category, nonverbal cues, have similar effects: They clearly indicate to the speaker the listener's attention and free both the speaker and listener from physical distractions and barriers that hinder interactions. The techniques of the third category, reflecting and clarifying techniques, are the most important in terms of verifying understanding, and these are also the most frequently omitted. Most miscommunication results from the speaker saying one thing and the listener hearing another. How often do children say, "You aren't listening to me!"? Adults are often not as open and hear from their own perspective without

Table 5.1   Communication Techniques

Listening	Nonverbal cues	Reflecting and clarifying
"Uh-huh."	Affirmative nods and smiles	"You're angry because . . ."
"OK."	Open body language, e.g., arms open	"You feel . . . because . . ."
"I'm following you."	Appropriate distance from speaker—not too close or too far	"You seem quite upset."
"For instance?"	Eye contact	"So, you would like . . ."
"And?"	Nondistracting environment	"I understand that you see the problem as . . ."
"Mmm."	Face speaker and lean forward	"I'm not sure, but I think you mean . . ."
"I understand."	Barrier-free space, e.g., desk not used as blocker	"I think you're saying . . ."
"This is great information for me."		
"Really?"		
"Then?"		
"So?"		
"Tell me more."		
"Go on."		
"I see."		
"Right."		

SOURCE: Sullivan/Glanz, *Supervision That Improves Teaching* (2005).

verifying. So many misunderstandings could be avoided through the use of these techniques.

Barriers to Communication

Another category comprises a set of reactions that have dele-terious consequences for both the listener and the speaker: They discourage people from expressing themselves openly; they interrupt and often end the narration; they put the speaker on the defensive; and they prevent the listener from hearing the speaker's perspective. These barriers to communication are referred to as "spoilers" and high-risk responses, and as a general rule they should be avoided (see Table 5.2.).

- *Foster cooperation, not competition.* When faculty compete with each other (for principal attention, for resources, etc.), they don't listen to each other, because heralding their own position is paramount. Competitive situations breed distrust. When you can develop mutual objectives and there's shared buy-in, a cooperative spirit ensues. Cooperation means members are dependent on one another. Uline et al. (2004) maintain, "When organizational participants recognize that they need the cooperation of other members, this awareness fosters open communication, resource exchange, perspective taking and mutual influence that tend to result in increased productivity" (p. 811).

- *Try a shared reading clinic.* Many books and articles of a somewhat controversial nature can be shared with faculty and staff. Use these works for discussion at grade and faculty conferences. As principal, your role is to facilitate discussion, encouraging diverse points of view and multiframed problem-solving strategies.

- *Learn to acknowledge your mistakes.* After you've made a decision about any educational matter, readily admit any errors you might have made, and realize that others may have more viable solutions to school problems than you do.

- *Force yourself to listen carefully.* Although you may have called the committee meeting and shared your vision with the participants, listen intently to the views of others. Take notes as they speak, use body language to indicate your attentiveness (e.g., nodding your head), and paraphrase their points.

- *Support shared governance opportunities.* Encourage others to aspire to democratic leadership by facilitating teacher empowerment

Table 5.2   Barriers to Communication

Barrier type	Examples
1. Judging	1. Judging
• Criticizing	• "You are lazy; your lesson plan is poor."
• Name calling and labeling	• "You are inexperienced, an intellectual."
• Diagnosing—analyzing motives instead of listening	• "You're taking out your anger on her."
	• "I know what you need."
• Praising evaluatively	• "You're terrific!"
2. Solutions	2. Solutions
• Ordering	• "You must . . ." "You have to . . ." "You will . . ."
• Threatening	• "If you don't . . ." "You had better or else."
• Moralizing or preaching	• "It is your duty/responsibility; you should . . ."
• Inappropriate questioning or prying	• "Why?" "What?" "How?" "When?"
• Advising	• "What I would do is . . ." "It would be best for you to . . ."
• Lecturing	• "Here is why you are wrong . . ." "Do you realize . . . ?"
3. Avoiding the other's concerns	3. Avoiding the other's concerns
• Diverting	• "Speaking of . . . " "Apropos . . . " "You know what happened to . . . ?"
• Reassuring	• "It's not so bad . . ." "You're lucky . . ." "You'll feel better."
• Withdrawing	• "I'm very busy . . ." "I can't talk right now . . ." "I'll get back to you . . ."
• Sarcasm	• "I really feel sorry for you."

SOURCE: Sullivan/Glanz, *Supervision That Improves Teaching* (2005).

and developing democratic structures and processes in a variety of school contexts (e.g., school-based leadership teams to revise curricula).

- *Serve as a buffer to the school bureaucracy.* You are people sensitive. Many people cannot confront the monolithic "steel monster" we call the "board of education." Frustrated and sometimes treated without compassion, people walk away from the school or district board with a distasteful experience. You can serve to mitigate such negative feelings. Treating people with dignity, respect, and caring comes easy to you. You represent the very best schools have to offer.

- *Bring out the best in others.* Your ability to influence and empower others lies deep within you. You understand the power of praise, of maintaining high expectations of others, of involving others in decision making, of granting professional autonomy, and of leading by standing behind. By leading by example, you have the potential to empower others (Blase & Kirby, 2000).

Reflective Question

1. What suggestions above made the most sense to you for dealing with conflict?

---

3. DEALING WITH THE CHALLENGE OF RENEWAL

All organizations need revitalization from time to time. Whether a school wallows in mediocrity because it becomes complacent with its successes or is in desperate need of curricular and instructional reform because of low student achievement levels, the issue of school renewal must be addressed by cultural leaders.

The concept of organizational renewal was first articulated by Rensis Likert (1961). Later extended by other theorists (Owens, 2004), the processes of renewal include:

- The capacity to identify problems as they emerge
- The establishment of goals, objectives, and priorities
- The ability to generate alternative solutions to a problem
- The ability to implement a solution and to monitor its success

School renewal processes attempt to address fundamental beliefs and values (i.e., culture) of a school while recognizing that ultimate success is dependent upon individuals within the school assuming responsibility for educational change (Owens, 2004).

According to Owens (2004), "a self-renewing school possesses three essential characteristics" (p. 222): a supportive culture that highly values problem solving, a clear set of strategies that facilitate problem solving, and a school that utilizes an array of resources to address its problems.

Here are some research-based strategies, among others, for constructively dealing with the challenge of school renewal:

- *Create a democratic learning community.* Imaginative leaders move the organization from "established practice" toward "emerging practice." Imagine new ways of viewing learning. Learning is no longer conceived as predictable but rather as a complex and differentiated process. Teaching moves from simple rote methods to informed reflective judgments. Supervision is no longer concerned with ensuring adherence to bureaucratic regulations but is concerned with helping teachers discover and construct professional knowledge and skills. Teachers and principals are no longer isolated and independent technicians but are collegial team members, mentors, and peer coaches. Schools are no longer bureaucratic teaching organizations but rather are democratic teaching and learning communities (Sergiovanni, 1996).

- *Set aside time for yourself.* You are always ready to help others, often at great personal expense. That's noble and very much needed, but you should realize that you are of no help to others if you don't care for yourself. Find time; don't plan too much. Be flexible and leave room for spontaneity. Take a minivacation in your office. Close your eyes and recall the wonderful, relaxed time you had on the Colorado rapids (Glanz, 2000).

- *Serve as a role model by encouraging collegiality.* Several individuals within the system will still try to adhere to the old industrial model based on an obedient workforce that was predisposed to following orders from above. Schools, as you know, are too complex for such isolated decision making to persist. You realize the importance of allowing others to assume more responsibility and to participate fully in shared decision making. Because you are people oriented, you should encourage others to work closely with their colleagues on instructional, curricular, and administrative matters. Avoiding impersonal or bureaucratic relationships in favor of encouraging personal relationships within a learning community can be one of your foremost contributions.

- *Engage in reflective practice.* Schon (1987) discusses a type of reflective thinking termed *reflection-on-action.* Reflection-on-action occurs when principals look back upon their work and consider thoughtfully what practices were successful and what areas need improvement. Too busy? Can't find the time? Try this suggestion, and you'll discover that problem solving can be enhanced: Schedule time on your calendar, during the least hectic time of day (e.g., 1:45–2:00 p.m.) to close your door, take the phone off the hook, and consider one area that requires careful consideration (e.g., "How might I best introduce this new instructional initiative?").

- *Undertake action research.* Action research is a powerful tool of disciplined inquiry that enables a principal to carefully and systematically reflect on practice and problem-solve. Follow these four easy steps: (a) select a focus of concern, (b) collect data, (c) analyze and interpret the data, and (d) take action. School renewal cannot occur without using action research as a basis for change and as a measure of success after reform implementation (Glanz, 2003).

- *Create a think tank.* Ideas are what drive an organization toward renewal and improvement. Generate ideas by establishing a "think tank" in your school. Identify a number of key individuals who possess great imagination. Gather them together for weekly or biweekly meetings. Identify specific areas of concern and brainstorm solutions. Bring the ideas generated to other faculty and staff for group consideration. Refine and crystallize the ideas. Develop a hypothesis or a set of research questions for field testing. Monitor progress, but always value the development of ideas.

Reflective Question

1. How else might you foster school renewal?

CONCLUSION

Cultural leaders are rarely satisfied. They are risk takers who aim to improve teaching and learning. They are visionary. They see the school as an organization and attempt to develop ways to improve practice. They have a good sense of what the school needs. They understand the inner workings of the school and know how to manipulate and "work the system" to ensure success. They aren't afraid of change. They embrace it and find ways to encourage others to discover new ways of doing things. Yet, they are not interested in ephemeral change or change for change's sake. Principals are serious about school improvement and seek research-based, proven ideas to enhance teaching and learning.

Also, principals aren't afraid of conflict. They know that conflict can inject energy into a stagnant system. Yet, they realize that conflict must be constructive in order to move the organization forward in positive ways. Renewing schools is the lifeblood of a cultural leader. The principal rallies teachers and others to examine their practices and find new and exciting ways to meet ever-changing student needs. Principals as cultural leaders retain the values and practices of the past that stand the test of time, but they are ready and willing to make the necessary changes to bring the school to the next level of success.

Change, conflict, and renewal are the realities of a cultural leader.

Conclusion

Building and Sustaining
a Learning Community

"Learning communities are concerned with growth and continuous self-renewal of both individuals and organizations. The leader is therefore responsible for building organizations where people are continually expanding their capabilities to shape their future—that is, leaders are responsible for learning."

—Gerald C. Ubben, Larry W. Hughes,
and Cynthia J. Norris

"Communitas, communis—to find what is held in common or shared by many."

—Latin root of the word *community*

As a cultural leader, you are aware that your role is fourfold:

- Sustaining positive organizational climate and culture
- Developing visionary leadership
- Promoting cultural diversity
- Fostering organizational self-renewal

Your ultimate goal, however, is to fully understand and utilize school culture in order to build and sustain a community that *values learning,* for students, educators, and community members alike. In other words, cultural leaders shape beliefs and values of members of the community in order to *emphasize learning above all else.*

Reflective Questions

1. What are some of the values, beliefs, and dispositions that you think are needed in a learning community?

2. Why is cultural leadership so critical a factor to build and sustain a learning community?

3. What knowledge, skills, and dispositions do effective cultural leaders possess?

4. Have you seen cultural leaders build and nurture strong communities for learning? Explain.

5. What can you do to specifically demonstrate your commitment to learning at all levels? Any symbols you can use as cultural leader?

Cultural leaders believe, as does Fullan (1995), that "quality learning for all students depends on quality learning for all educators" (p. 5). That includes, by the way, you as the principal. If you are to make a difference in the academic and social lives of students, you must be exposed to and participate in quality learning not only in your own preparation programs but on the job as well. If schools are to make a difference in our post-9/11 society, the building of a community of staff and student learners must be a primary goal for us. Excellence and quality in education are no longer utopian ideals but are urgently needed to adequately prepare and equip learners for a global postindustrial society "characterized by exponential information growth, fast-paced innovation, organizational change, and participatory democracy" (Ambrose & Cohen, 1997, p. 20).

According to Fullan (1995), quality learning depends on the "development of the six interrelated domains of teaching and learning, collegiality, context expertise, continuous learning, change process, and moral purpose" (pp. 5–6). As Figure 6.1 illustrates, all of us need to do the following:

- Understand that teaching is complex and textual (Hare, 1993), that teachers are facilitators of learning (Joyce & Weil, 1999), and that learning occurs when learners construct meaning on their own (Cochran, DeRuiter, & King, 1993)
- Value collegial relationships and participate as active members in a democratic learning community (e.g., Goodlad, 1994; Sergiovanni, 1994)
- Demonstrate a commitment to specific knowledge, understanding, and skills needed for relating to and taking account of parents, communities, businesses, and social agencies (Fullan, 1995) and therefore appreciate and consider all aspects of cultural diversity among students and community (Nieto, 2003)
- Develop intellectual and emotional habits of critical reflection (reflective analysis) and action about our professional work (LaBoskey, 1994), realizing that the mark of a professional is exhibited in a sustained effort of self-improvement (Goodlad, 1994)
- Tolerate ambiguity, remain flexible, and be willing to take risks (Ambrose & Cohen, 1997), realizing that in a complex, ever-changing world, we must not only cope with unpredictable events and trends but must become agents of change in our own right
- Believe that we make a difference in the lives of all students academically (Cotton, 2003) and that we are driven by a moral purpose that affirms human dignity and a sense of caring for all people (Noddings, 1984, 1986, 1992)

TEACHING AND LEARNING

As principal, you realize that the knowledge base for teachers is more varied and complex than ever before. Teachers must draw on multiple teaching strategies to meet a wide range of individual needs. They must understand how diverse, multiethnic students

Figure 6.1   Educator (Principal) Development Domains

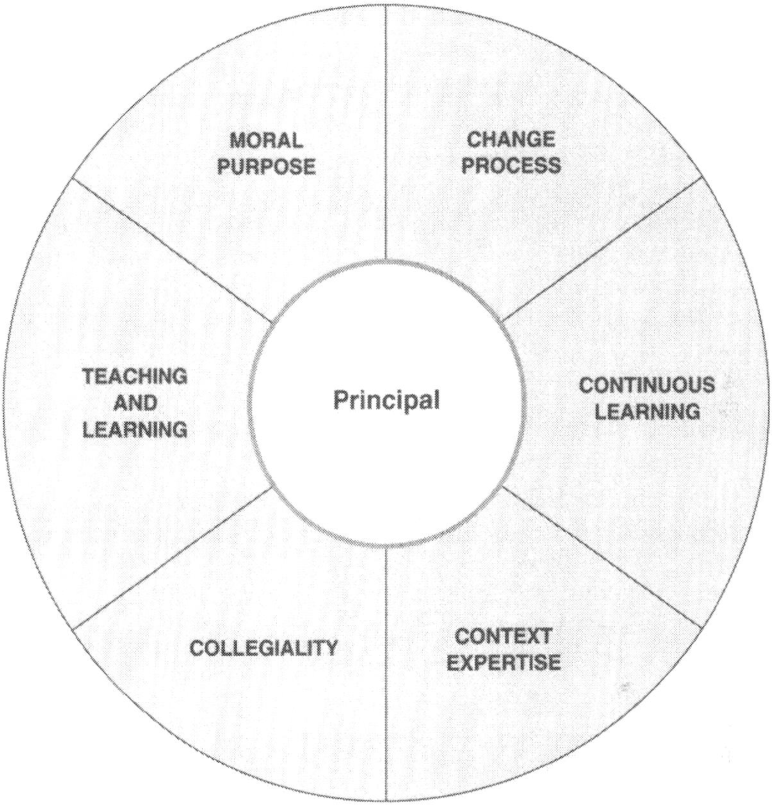

learn and must be skilled in technological applications. They must also possess knowledge of assessment and monitoring techniques to better frame instruction and curriculum.

Teachers need to be prepared for learner-centered schools in which classrooms are humane, interactive, and intellectually rigorous places. Teachers are concerned with preparing students who themselves are knowledgeable, have requisite academic and social skills, and appreciate the value of lifelong learning. The pursuit of these more challenging approaches to teaching and learning requires strong principal leadership and changes in curricula, school organization, and professional development.

COLLEGIALITY

As schools more and more move away from traditional forms of school organization, increased demands for reconceptualizing curriculum and instruction are being heard. Principals now must work closely with other colleagues on instructional, curricular, and administrative matters. In participatory democracies, principals need to be capable of collegial problem solving in the face of complex issues. The cultural leader understands that the old model of "principal on a white horse" single-handedly solving a school's problems is no longer acceptable, if it ever was.

CONTEXT EXPERTISE

Effective principals must demonstrate active involvement in multiple contexts (multicultural and global) and positive interactions in multiple communities (families and agencies). Fullan (1995) states that "leadership and development also means becoming experts in context" (p. 7). This means, according to Fullan, developing expertise in "specific knowledge, understanding, and skills, needed for relating to and taking into account parents, communities, businesses, and social agencies" (p. 7). Becoming experts in context includes "specific strategies for connecting parents to learning, for learning to teach for cultural diversity, and for partnering with other educative agencies and institutions" (p. 7).

CONTINUOUS LEARNING

Reflective practice is a prime vehicle for principal continuous learning. Principals realize the importance of reflective practice in refining their unique knowledge, skills, and dispositions. Principals are aware of the importance of continuous learning not only to stay abreast of the latest developments in the field but also to continually seek self-improvement.

Table 6.1 Comparison of Old and New Paradigms of the Six Domains

Domains	Old paradigm	New paradigm
Teaching and learning	• Teaching is simple. • Principals are experts. • Knowledge is transferred to students.	• Teaching is complex. • Principals are facilitators. • Knowledge is constructed by learners from experience.
Collegiality	Impersonal/bureaucratic relationships prevail.	Personal relationships are fostered within a learning community.
Context expertise	Principals work in isolation of others.	Principals create multiple connections in which diversity is appreciated and fostered.
Continuous learning	Focus is on the improvement of learner.	Focus is on the growth of the principal as well.
Change process	Things are fixed, predictable, and unambiguous.	Things are complex, unpredictable, and ambiguous (chaos theory).
Moral purpose	Individual feels disempowered. Individual is subservient to organization.	Self-efficacy is affirmed and individuality valued.

CHANGE PROCESS

Principals certainly need knowledge and skills for understanding and adapting to the dynamics of change. More specifically, principals must know how to initiate change and how to manage change as it naturally occurs within and without the school organization. They must realize that the process of change, which is chaotic and unpredictable, is a natural state of affairs.

MORAL PURPOSE

Society, for many, is in a state of moral crisis. Maintaining high ideals and commitment is an important professional responsibility of principals. If principals are to develop a strong sense of ethics, they must be able to "appreciate the moral-ethical implications of multiple perspectives on complex issues, and to creatively synthesize these perspectives into viable solutions" (Ambrose & Cohen, 1997, p. 21). Principals as cultural leaders who deal most fundamentally with values must maintain a firm moral grounding.

COMPARING OLD AND NEW PARADIGMS

Table 6.1 summarizes the six domains and compares current thinking with old belief paradigms (refer back to Chapter 5's brief discussion of paradigms).

Cultural leaders think, believe, and work in the "new paradigm."

Reflective Questions

1. How might you work with these six domains as a cultural leader in your school?

2. What kinds of symbols might you use to convey your support for developing and sustaining a schoolwide learning community?

Resource A

Realities of Cultural Leadership:
In-Basket Simulations

T his section highlights some of the realities of cultural leadership using an approach called "In-Basket Simulations." It is a study technique derived from an approach used when I studied for licensure as a principal in New York City. The approach was developed by the Institute for Research and Professional Development (http://www.nycenet.edu/opm/opm/profservices/rfp1b723.html). Scenarios that you might encounter as a principal are presented for your reaction. For instance, "A letter from an irate parent complaining that her child is intentionally being ignored by the teacher during instruction in class is sent to your attention. What would you do?" Challenging you to confront real-life phenomena under controlled conditions, these simulated in-basket items will prompt critical inquiry.

Here are suggestions to guide you as you complete these in-basket exercises:

1. Think and respond as if you are a principal, not a teacher or perhaps an assistant principal.

2. Place yourself mentally in each situation as if the case were actually happening to you.

3. Draw on your experiences and from what you've learned from others. Think of a principal you respect, and ask yourself, "What would Mr. or Ms. X have done?"

4. Make distinctions between actions you would personally take and actions you would delegate to others.

5. Utilize resources (personnel or otherwise) to assist you.

6. Think about your response, and then share it with a colleague for her or his reaction.

7. Record your response, and then a day later reread the scenario and your response. Would you still have reacted the same way?

During an interview you are asked to respond to the following scenarios:

• The previous principal was removed for what the superintendent called "incompetence." Yet, the majority of the school faculty "loved" the principal because he was "easygoing" and infrequently observed teachers. You are the newly assigned principal to this school, in which reading and math standardized test scores have dropped precipitously over the past 3 years. Many of the teachers have worked in a culture that gave them almost carte blanche over instructional, curricular, and other school decisions. What are your short- and long-term goals, and how do you intend to reverse the climate that prevails?

• The former principal was a bureaucrat par excellence. You believe, in contrast, in building collaborative partnerships that encourage shared decision making. What will be your greatest challenges, and what steps would you take to introduce participatory school management?

• How would you forge a role for yourself as a cultural leader and not merely a manager or technician?

• Name the concrete and specific steps you would take to achieve each of the following:
    1. Build stronger, more trusting relationships with students
    2. Build trusting relationships with teachers
    3. Nurture an ethic of caring schoolwide

4. Build staff morale
5. Actualize your vision for the school
6. Lead in culturally relevant ways
7. Resolve conflicts between two faculty members

• Your vision to institute schoolwide inclusion is being met with much resistance by many teachers and parents. Yet, you remain committed to inclusion. What immediate steps could you take to move your vision forward? How will you deal with teacher and parent resistance? One parent adamantly proclaims, "Under no circumstances will I allow my child in a class with 'them.'"

• You are a principal in an ethnically diverse school. All the African American students sit by themselves in the cafeteria. What's your reaction? What would you do, if anything, to foster intergroup interaction, respect, and cooperation?

• A teacher in your school chastises a student for not looking at her in the "eyes" when posing a question. The matter comes to your attention. What would you do or say?

• A new balanced literacy program is mandated by the district. Teachers refuse to change the way they have been teaching. How do you introduce the new approach without ostracizing the teachers or ignoring their feelings?

• The chairperson of the math department has a verbal dispute with one of the school's senior teachers. The teacher then resigns, as do three other teachers in the department, leaving the department half-staffed. The four teachers, unbeknownst to you, all secure positions in another district. How do you deal with the conflict that ensues, and what do you do or say to the chairperson?

• You respond to an ad that reads, in part, "Principal wanted: A strategic thinker, leader and manager who will embrace a clear vision of the WayneBrook Elementary School's future that distinguishes its programs and services from other schools in the region. . . . A strong commitment to working in a diverse and multicultural community is essential." What would you say during the interview to demonstrate that you are the person for the position?

Don't forget to share responses with colleagues, because good discussion about these cultural issues will clarify your thoughts, expose you to viewpoints different from your own, and raise even more questions for consideration.

Resource B

Assessing Your Role as Cultural Leader

A s the principal, you realize a positive or healthy school climate is conducive to higher levels of faculty morale and student and parent satisfaction. You also realize the important role you play in enhancing or improving organizational climate. You are in a pivotal position to shape school culture, which in turn affects school and classroom climate and the overall health of your organization. Please take the survey below, because it will *serve as an important reflective tool to determine the relative health of your school and the steps you might need to take to reinvigorate the school culture and climate.* Please note that your responses are private. Therefore, your honest responses to the various items below will serve you best *as reflective tools to assist you in becoming an even better cultural leader.*

SA = Strongly Agree ("For the most part, yes.")
A = Agree ("Yes, but . . .")
D = Disagree ("No, but . . .")
SD = Strongly Disagree ("For the most part, no.")

SA   A   D   SD   1. Teachers willingly volunteer to serve
                       on school-based decision-making teams
                       and other grade or schoolwide
                       committees.

SA   A   D   SD   2. Teachers display enthusiasm and
                       commitment to school goals and
                       objectives.

SA   A   D   SD   3. A feeling of togetherness pervades the grade or school.

SA   A   D   SD   4. School governance is characterized by teachers as democratic participants.

SA   A   D   SD   5. Teachers are encouraged by the principal to get involved in decision making.

SA   A   D   SD   6. Teachers are aware of the school's mission and goals.

SA   A   D   SD   7. A problem-solving ethos pervades the school.

SA   A   D   SD   8. The principal takes the lead in setting a positive tone (i.e., friendliness and supportive environment).

SA   A   D   SD   9. Teachers fear change.

SA   A   D   SD   10. Teachers and principal work as a learning team.

SA   A   D   SD   11. Teachers feel threatened by the principal's presence.

SA   A   D   SD   12. Teachers are suspicious of the principal's motives.

SA   A   D   SD   13. Parents are not welcome in the school building.

SA   A   D   SD   14. Teachers encourage parental involvement by word and deed.

SA   A   D   SD   15. A pessimistic atmosphere pervades the school.

SA   A   D   SD   16. The principal is upbeat and positive (i.e., sees the glass as half full).

SA A D SD 17. Teachers articulate that they are proud of their accomplishments.

SA A D SD 18. Teachers' opinions are solicited and are used to shape school policy.

SA A D SD 19. Policies and procedures related to teachers are fair and equitable.

SA A D SD 20. Policies and procedures related to students are fair and equitable.

SA A D SD 21. Policies and procedures related to parents are fair and equitable.

SA A D SD 22. Lines of communication between parents and teachers are open.

SA A D SD 23. Innovative teaching practices are encouraged.

SA A D SD 24. When problems emerge, established procedures are in place to address them.

SA A D SD 25. The principal encourages risk taking and change.

SA A D SD 26. Parents are welcome in the classroom, at appropriate times.

SA A D SD 27. Parents are aware of the school's goals.

SA A D SD 28. Students are aware of the school's goals.

SA A D SD 29. Teachers enjoy getting together informally.

SA A D SD 30. Faculty take pride in each other's accomplishments.

SA A D SD 31. The principal is insecure and uncertain about how to plan for the future.

SA   A   D   SD   32. Teachers trust the principal.

SA   A   D   SD   33. Students trust the principal.

SA   A   D   SD   34. Parents trust the principal.

SA   A   D   SD   35. The principal is accessible to parents.

SA   A   D   SD   36. The principal is accessible to teachers.

SA   A   D   SD   37. The principal is accessible to students.

SA   A   D   SD   38. The principal tries to cover up problems.

SA   A   D   SD   39. The principal solicits and values the opinions of others.

SA   A   D   SD   40. Workshops are planned collaboratively.

SA   A   D   SD   41. Teachers' opinions are solicited and used to improve the school in some way.

SA   A   D   SD   42. Student misbehavior goes unpunished.

SA   A   D   SD   43. The principal is generally well liked by teachers.

SA   A   D   SD   44. The principal is pleasant, cooperative, and supportive of teachers.

SA   A   D   SD   45. The principal is a strong advocate of student rights.

SA   A   D   SD   46. Rules and regulations are applied fairly and judiciously.

SA   A   D   SD   47. Most parents support school policies.

SA A D SD 48. The school has an outstanding reputation in the community.

SA A D SD 49. The principal cares for teachers' feelings.

SA A D SD 50. The principal supports teachers in student disciplinary matters.

SA A D SD 51. Students enjoy coming to school.

SA A D SD 52. Teachers enjoy coming to school.

SA A D SD 53. The principal rewards teachers for going beyond the call of duty.

SA A D SD 54. The principal is blatantly prejudiced.

SA A D SD 55. Innovations are encouraged.

SA A D SD 56. Students are involved in decision making.

SA A D SD 57. Students report that they have a feeling of belonging to the school community.

SA A D SD 58. Students keep their classrooms, corridor, and school building clean (e.g., clean of graffiti).

SA A D SD 59. The principal, by word and deed, supports cultural diversity.

SA A D SD 60. The principal maintains high expectations for performance and emphasizes instructional excellence.

Analyzing your responses:

This survey is not meant to serve as the final assessment of positive school culture and climate. Rather, several research-based categories that reflect positive culture and climate are covered in order to enable you to consider best practices. Below, each category is identified and briefly explained, and the survey statement numbers that correspond to a category are noted. Overlap of items can occur.

Indicators of positive school climate: Although all survey items in some way relate to school culture and climate, the following statements are particularly relevant: 8, 15, 16, 17, 30, 31, 38, 43, 44, 45, 47, 48, 51, 52, 58, 60.

Parental involvement: A positive school culture and climate is attained when parents actively and constructively take part in school activities, as indicated by the following statements: 13, 14, 22, 26, 27, 34, 35, 39.

Problem-solving strategies: A problem-solving ethos is a strong indicator of positive climate, as the following statements address: 7, 24.

Risk-taking strategies: Principals encourage innovation, a hallmark of positive school culture and climate, as indicated in the following statements: 9, 23, 25, 55.

Teacher involvement: Positive school climate is influenced by the nature and degree of teacher involvement in school affairs, as indicated in the following statements: 1, 2, 4, 5, 6, 18, 36, 39, 40, 41.

Team approach: Schools that encourage a team approach to planning, implementing, and evaluating school activities and programs are indicative of positive school culture and climate, as indicated in the following statements: 3, 10.

Principal-teacher relationship: High morale and positive climate are affected by the nature and extent of the teacher-principal relationship, as indicated in the following statements: 11, 12, 32, 53.

Student involvement: Positive school climate is influenced by the nature and degree of student involvement in school affairs, as indicated in the following statements: 28, 33, 37, 39, 56, 57.

Social justice: Positive school climate is achieved when principals address and advocate justice for all students, parents, and teachers, as indicated in the following statements: 19, 20, 21, 46, 54, 59.

Teachers supported: Teachers report positive school climate when they are supported by the principal's words and deeds, as indicated in the following statements: 42, 44, 49, 50.

Reflective Questions

1. How might you use survey explanations to assess your school's culture and climate?

2. What insights into culture and climate have you gained from this exercise?

3. Examine each category and corresponding statement, and explain how you intend to actively change your behavior in order to best promote positive school climate.

Resource C

An Annotated Bibliography
of Best Resources

T he literature on the principalship and related areas is extensive. The list below is not meant to serve as a comprehensive resource by any means. The selected titles I have annotated are few but, in my opinion, are among the most useful references on the subject. Rather than "impress" you with a more extensive list, I have selected these outstanding works related specifically to cultural leadership that will supplement my book quite well. I may have missed, of course, many other important works. Nevertheless, the list below is a good start. Don't forget that life is a long journey of continuous learning. Continue to hone your skills by reading good books and journal articles on cultural leadership. No one is ever perfect, and everyone can learn something new by keeping current with the literature in the field. Share your readings and reactions with a colleague.

Cultural Leadership

Beaudoin, M. N., & Taylor, M. (2004). *Creating a positive school culture: How principals and teachers can solve problems together.* Thousand Oaks, CA: Corwin.

A practical guidebook that is simple to read but packed with lots of useful ideas.

Bolman, L. G., & Deal, T. E. (2003). *Reframing organizations: Artistry, choice, and leadership* (3rd ed.). San Francisco: Jossey-Bass.

Classic in the field; a must-read. Four ways or frames of viewing organizations are presented: structural frame, human resource frame, political frame, and symbolic frame.

Cunningham, W. G., & Gresso, D. W. (1993). *Cultural leadership: The culture of excellence in education.* Boston: Allyn & Bacon.

One of the most comprehensive treatments of school culture and leadership. Topics include, among others, visionary leadership, professional development, and school transformation.

Deal, T. E., & Peterson, K. D. (2003). *Shaping school culture: The heart of leadership.* San Francisco: Jossey-Bass.

Perhaps the most important resource to read on principal cultural leadership. If you could read only one work, then this would be the one I recommend. Filled with stories, anecdotes, cases, and strategies, this book addresses the complexities and dynamics of school culture in all its facets.

Fullan, M. (2003). *Leading in a culture of change.* San Francisco: Jossey-Bass.

Organizational change and leadership strategies are conveyed simply yet without undermining the complexities of change that a cultural leader must understand.

Lindsey, R. B., Roberts, L. M., & CampbellJones, F. (2005). *The culturally proficient school: An implementation guide for school leaders.* Thousand Oaks, CA: Corwin.

A superb guide for principals who want to put cultural proficiency into action schoolwide.

Lindsey, R. B., Terrell, R. D., & Robins, K. N. (2003). *Cultural proficiency: A manual for school leaders* (2nd ed.). Thousand Oaks, CA: Corwin.

An excellent resource for principals, this work deals in depth with cultural diversity challenges in schools.

Schein, E. H. (1996). *Organizational culture and leadership.* San Francisco: Jossey-Bass.

One of the most often quoted sources on cultural leadership. Although Schein deals with nonschool settings, by and large, his descriptions are relevant for our work as principals.

Related Classics in Leadership

Fullan, M. (Ed.). (2000). *The Jossey-Bass reader: Educational leadership.* San Francisco: Jossey-Bass.

Collection of useful essays by leading authorities on organizational behavior, the principalship, diversity, moral and shared leadership, and so on.

Glickman, C. D. (2003). *Holding sacred ground: Essays on leadership, courage, and endurance in our schools.* San Francisco: Jossey-Bass.

Useful compilation of essays for the cultural school leader.

Senge, P. M. (1990). *The fifth discipline.* New York: Doubleday.

Senge's books are classic and must be read by principals. Although he talks about corporate America, his views on "systems thinking" to help institutions become "learning organizations" are most relevant to our work in schools. His views on culture and visionary leadership are particularly helpful.

School Renewal

Glickman, C. D. (2003). *Renewing America's schools: A guide for school-based action.* San Francisco: Jossey-Bass.

Uplifting guide with practical examples from schools.

Hansen, J. H., & Lifton, E. (1999). *Leadership for continuous school improvement.* Swampscott, MA: Watersun.

Although not very well known, this work is superb for its simplicity, breadth, and practical usefulness.

Starratt, R. J. (1995). *Leaders with vision: The quest for school renewal.* Thousand Oaks, CA: Corwin.

A small volume, a bit dense at times, but nonetheless intelligently woven and a necessary read for any cultural leader who aims to improve schools.

References

Ambrose, D., & Cohen, L. M. (1997). The post-industrial era: Finding the giftedness in all children. *Focus on Education, 41,* 20–23.

Anyon, J. (1981). Social class and the hidden curriculum of work. In H. A. Giroux, A. N. Penn, & W. F. Pinar (Eds.), *Curriculum and instruction: Alternatives in education.* Berkeley, CA: McCutchan.

Apple, M. (1986). *Teachers and text: A political economy of class and gender.* London: Routledge.

Argyris, C. (1957). *Personality and organization.* New York: Harper & Row.

Banks, J. (1997). *Educating citizens in a multicultural society.* New York: Teachers College Press.

Beck, L. G. (1994). *Reclaiming educational administration as a caring profession.* New York: Teachers College Press.

Beck, L. G., & Murphy, J. (1993). *Understanding the principalship: Metaphorical themes, 1920s–1990s.* New York: Teachers College Press.

Bennis, W. G. (1989). *Why leaders can't lead.* San Francisco: Jossey-Bass.

Blackmore, J. (1993). In the shadow of man: The historical construction of educational administration as a "masculinist" enterprise. In J. Blackmore & J. Kenway (Eds.), *Gender matters in educational administration and policy* (pp. 27–48). London: Falmer.

Blanchard, K. H., & Johnson, S. (1983). *The one minute manager.* New York: William Morrow and Company.

Blase, J., & Kirby, P. C. (2000). *Bringing out the best in teachers: What effective principals do.* Thousand Oaks, CA: Corwin.

Blau, P. M., & Meyer, M. W. (1987). *Bureaucracy in modern society.* New York: Random House.

Blumberg, A. (1980). *Supervisors and teachers: A private cold war.* New York: McCutchan.

Boyer, J. B., & Baptiste, H. P., Jr. (1996). *Transforming the curriculum for multicultural understandings: A practitioner's handbook.* San Francisco: Caddo Gap Press.

Bryson, B. (2003). *A short history of nearly everything.* New York: Broadway.

Callahan, R. E. (1962). *Education and the cult of efficiency.* Chicago: University of Chicago Press.

Callahan, R. E. (1996). Foreword. *Peabody Journal of Education, 71*(2), 1–14.

Cochran, K. F., DeRuiter, J. A., & King, R. A. (1993). Pedagogical content knowing: An integrative model for teacher preparation. *Journal of Teacher Education, 44,* 263–272.

Cotton, K. (2003). *Principals and student achievement: What research says.* Alexandria, VA: Association for Supervision and Curriculum Development.

Danielson, C. (2002). *Enhancing student achievement: A framework for school improvement.* Alexandria, VA: Association for Supervision and Curriculum Development.

Deal, T. E., & Peterson, K. D. (1999). *Shaping school culture: The heart of leadership.* San Francisco: Jossey-Bass.

DeRoche, E. F. (1987). *An administrator's guide for evaluating programs and personnel: An effective schools approach.* Boston: Allyn & Bacon.

Dunn, D. (1995). *Exploring social relationships.* Englewood Cliffs, NJ: Prentice Hall.

Elliott, D., & McKenney, M. (1998). Four inclusion models that work. *Teaching Exceptional Children, 28,* 54–58.

Etzioni, A. (1975). *A comparative analysis of complex organizations.* New York: Free Press.

Evans, R. (2004). *Family matters: How schools can cope with the crisis of childrearing.* San Francisco: Jossey-Bass.

Ferguson, K. E. (1984). *The feminist case against bureaucracy.* Philadelphia: Temple University Press.

Fiedler, F. E., & Chemers, M. M. (1984). *Improving leadership effectiveness.* New York: Wiley.

Fox, R. S., & Boies, H. E. (n.d.). *School climate improvement: A challenge to the school administrator.* Bloomington, IN: Phi Delta Kappan.

Fullan, M. (1995). Division I introduction—Contexts: Overview and framework. In M. J. O'Hair & S. J. Odell (Eds.), *Educating teachers for leadership and change* (pp. 1–10). Thousand Oaks, CA: Corwin.

Fullan, M. (1997). *What's worth fighting for in the principalship.* New York: Teachers College Press.

Giroux, H. A. (Ed.). (1991). *Postmodernism, feminism, and cultural politics.* Albany: State University of New York Press.

Glanz, J. (1998a). Images of principals in film and television: From Mr. Wameke to Mr. Rivelle to Mr. Woodman. *Journal of Educational Leadership and Administration, 10,* 7–24.

Glanz, J. (1998b). Multicultural education as a moral imperative: Affirming the diversity of ideas and perspectives. *Focus on Education, 42,* 18–24.

Glanz, J. (2000). *Relax for success: A practical guide for educators to relieve stress.* Norwood, MA: Christopher-Gordon.

Glanz, J. (2002). *Finding your leadership style: A guide for educators.* Alexandria, VA: Association for Supervision and Curriculum Development.

Glanz, J. (2003). *Action research: An educational leader's guide to school improvement* (2nd ed.). Norwood, MA: Christopher-Gordon.

Glanz, J., & Behar-Horenstein, L. (2000). *Paradigm debates in curriculum and supervision: Modern and postmodern perspectives.* Westport, CT: Bergin & Garvey.

Glasser, W. A. (1975). *Reality therapy.* New York: HarperCollins.

Glickman, C. D., & Mells, R. (1997). Why is advocacy for diversity in appointing supervisory leaders a moral imperative? In J. Glanz & R. F. Neville (Eds.), *Educational supervision: Perspectives, issues, and controversies* (pp. 341–352). Norwood, MA: Christopher-Gordon.

Goodlad, J. I. (1994). *Educational renewal.* San Francisco: Jossey-Bass.

Green, R. L. (2005). *Practicing the art of leadership.* Upper Saddle River, NJ: Pearson.

Hare, W. (1993). *What makes a good teacher: Reflections on some characteristics central to the educational enterprise.* London, Ontario, Canada: Althouse.

Harris, S. (2004). *The end of faith: Religion, terror, and the future of reason.* New York: W. W. Norton.

Henry, M. (1996). *Parent-school collaboration: Feminist organizational structures and school leadership.* Albany: State University of New York Press.

Hersey, P., & Blanchard, K. (1988). *Management of organizational behavior.* Englewood Cliffs, NJ: Prentice Hall.

Herzberg, F. (1966). *Work and the nature of man.* Cleveland, OH: Cleveland World.

Johnson, S., & Blanchard, K. H. (1998). *Who moved my cheese? An amazing way to deal with change in your work and in your life.* New York: Putnam.

Jordan Irvine, J. J., & Armento, B. J. (2003). *Culturally responsive teaching.* Boston: McGraw-Hill.

Joyce, B., & Weil, M. (1999). *Models of teaching* (6th ed.). Boston: Allyn & Bacon.

Kochhar, C. A., West, L. L., & Taymans, J. M. (2000). *Successful inclusion: Practical strategies for a shared responsibility.* Upper Saddle River, NJ: Merrill.

Kottler, E., & Kottler, J. A. (2002). *Children with limited English: Teaching strategies for the regular classroom.* Thousand Oaks, CA: Corwin.

Kozol, J. (1991). *Savage inequalities.* New York: Crown.

LaBoskey, V. (1994). *Development of reflective practice.* New York: Teachers College Press.

Likert, R. (1961). *New patterns of management.* New York: McGraw-Hill.

Lindsey, R. B., Roberts, L. M., & CampbellJones, F. (2005). *The culturally proficient school: An implementation guide for school leaders.* Thousand Oaks, CA: Corwin.

Lindsey, R. B., Robins, L., & Terrell, R. D. (2003). *Cultural proficiency: A manual for school leaders* (2nd ed.). Thousand Oaks, CA: Corwin.

Lunenburg, F. C., & Ornstein, A. C. (2003). *Educational administration: Concepts and practices.* Belmont, CA: Wadsworth.

Marshall, C. (1995). Imagining leadership. *Educational Administration Quarterly, 31,* 484–492.

Marshall, C., Patterson, J. A., Rogers, D. L., & Steele, J. R. (1996). Caring as career: An alternative perspective for educational administration. *Educational Administration Quarterly, 32,* 271–294.

Maslow, A. (1970). *Motivation and personality.* New York: Harper & Row.

Matthews, L. J., & Crow, G. M. (2003). *Being and becoming a principal: Role conceptions for contemporary principals and principals.* Boston: Allyn & Bacon.

McLeskey, J., & Waldron, N. (2001). *Inclusive schools in action: Making differences ordinary.* Alexandria, VA: Association for Supervision and Curriculum Development.

Morse, T. E. (2002). Designing appropriate curriculum for special education students in urban schools. *Education and Urban Society, 35*(1), 4–17.

Neusner, J. (Ed.). (2003). *World religions in America: An introduction.* Louisville, KY: Westminster John Knox Press.

Nieto, S. (2003). *Affirming diversity* (4th ed.). New York: Longman.

Noddings, N. (1984). *Caring: A feminist approach to ethics and moral education.* Berkeley: University of California Press.

Noddings, N. (1986). Fidelity in teaching, teacher education, and research for teaching. *Harvard Educational Review, 56,* 496–510.

Noddings, N. (1992). *The challenge to care in schools: An alternative approach to education.* New York: Teachers College Press.

Oakes, J. (1985). *Keeping track: How schools structure inequality.* New Haven, CT: Yale University Press.

Ogbu, J. (1978). *Minority education and the caste: The American system in cross cultural perspective.* San Diego, CA: Academic Press.

Osterman, K. E., & Kottkamp, R. B. (1993). *Reflective practice for educators: Improving schooling through professional development.* Thousand Oaks, CA: Corwin.

Osterman, K. E., & Kottkamp, R. B. (2004). *Reflective practice for educators: Improving schooling through professional development* (2nd ed.). Thousand Oaks, CA: Corwin.

Owens, R. G. (1995). *Organizational behavior in education* (5th ed.). Boston: Allyn & Bacon.

Owens, R. G. (2004). *Organizational behavior in education* (8th ed.). Boston: Allyn & Bacon.

Owings, W. A., & Kaplan, L. S. (Eds.). (2003). *Best practices, best thinking, and emerging issues in school leadership.* Thousand Oaks, CA: Corwin.

Portin, B. (with Schneider, P., DeArmond, M., & Gundlach, L.). (2003). *Making sense of leading schools: A study of the school principalship.* Retrieved February 19, 2005, from http://www.crpe.org/pubs/pdf/MakingSense_PortinWeb.pdf

Ravitch, D. (1995). *National standards in American education: A citizen's guide.* Washington, DC: Brookings Institution.

Regan, H. B. (1990). Not for women only: School administration as a feminist activity. *Teachers College Record, 91*, 565–577.

Roberts, S., & Pruitt, E. (2003). *Schools as professional learning communities.* Thousand Oaks, CA: Corwin.

Rogers, C. R. (1951). *Client-centered therapy.* Boston: Houghton Mifflin.

Rosenthal, R., & Jacobson, L. (1968). *Pygmalion in the classroom: Teacher expectation and pupils' intellectual development.* New York: Rinehart and Winston.

Sadker, M., & Sadker, D. (1994). *Failing at fairness: How our schools cheat girls.* New York: Simon & Schuster.

Sarason, S. B. (1996). *Revisiting "The culture of the school and the problem of change."* New York: Teachers College Press.

Schein, E. H. (1992). *Organizational culture and leadership* (2nd ed.). San Francisco: Jossey-Bass.

Schon, D. A. (1987). *Educating the reflective practitioner: Toward a new design for thinking and learning in the professions.* San Francisco: Jossey-Bass.

Sergiovanni, T. J. (1992). *Moral leadership: Getting to the heart of school improvement.* San Francisco: Jossey-Bass.

Sergiovanni, T. J. (1994). *Building community in schools.* San Francisco: Jossey-Bass.

Sergiovanni, T. J. (1996). *Leadership for the schoolhouse: How is it different? Why is it important?* San Francisco: Jossey-Bass.

Sergiovanni, T. J., & Starratt, R. J. (1997). *Supervision: A redefinition.* New York: McGraw-Hill.

Skinner, B. F. (1976). *Walden two.* Englewood Cliffs, NJ: Prentice Hall.

Sowell, T. (1996). *Migration and culture.* New York: Basic Books.

Sowell, T. (2002). *A conflicting vision: Ideological origins of political struggles.* New York: Basic Books.

Spring, J. (1994). *The American school, 1642–1993* (3rd ed.). New York: McGraw-Hill.

Starratt, R. J. (1991). Building an ethical school: A theory for practice in educational leadership. *Educational Administration Quarterly, 27,* 185–202.

Stolp, S. (1991). *Leadership for school culture* (Report No. 91). Eugene, OR: ERIC Clearinghouse on Educational Management. (ERIC Document Reproduction Service No. ED370198)

Strober, M. M., & Tyack, D. B. (1980). Why do women teach and men manage? A report on research on schools. *Signs, 5*(3), 494–503.

Sullivan, S., & Glanz, J. (2005). *Supervision that improves teaching: Strategies and techniques* (2nd ed.). Thousand Oaks, CA: Corwin.

Sullivan, S., & Glanz, J. (2006). *Building effective learning communities: Strategies for leadership, learning, & collaboration.* Thousand Oaks, CA: Corwin.

Tauber, R. T. (1997). *Self-fulfilling prophecy: A practical guide to its use in education.* Westport, CT: Praeger.

Totten, S., & Feinberg, S. (2000). *Teaching and studying the Holocaust.* Boston: Allyn & Bacon.

Uline, C. L., Tschannen-Moran, M., & Perez, L. (2004). Constructive conflict: How controversy can contribute to school improvement. *Teachers College Record, 105,* 782–816.

Weiss, J. (1997). *Ideology of death: Why the Holocaust happened in Germany.* New York: Ivan R. Dee.

Whyte, W. H. (1956). *The organization man.* New York: Simon & Schuster.

Wilmore, E. L. (2002). *Principal leadership: Applying the new Educational Leadership Constituent Council (ELCC) standards.* Thousand Oaks, CA: Corwin.

Wolfendale, S. (2000). *Special needs in the early years: Snapshots of practice.* London: Routledge.

Zittleman, K., & Sadker, D. (n.d.). *Teacher education textbooks: The unfinished gender revolution.* Retrieved March 15, 2005, from http://www.sadker.org/textbooks.htm

Index

Note: Page references marked *t* are tables; those marked *f* are figures

**CORWIN
PRESS**

The Corwin Press logo—a raven striding across an open book—represents the union of courage and learning. Corwin Press is committed to improving education for all learners by publishing books and other professional development resources for those serving the field of PreK–12 education. By providing practical, hands-on materials, Corwin Press continues to carry out the promise of its motto: **"Helping Educators Do Their Work Better."**

Made in the USA
Lexington, KY
19 March 2012